From **INSPIRATION**
To **RED CARPET**

Host Your Own
Student Film Festival

William L. Bass
Christian Goodrich
Kim Lindskog

International Society for Technology in Education
EUGENE, OREGON • WASHINGTON, DC

From **INSPIRATION** to **RED CARPET**

Host Your Own **Student Film Festival**

William L. Bass, Christian Goodrich, and Kim Lindskog

Director of Book Publishing: *Courtney Burkholder*
Acquisitions Editor: *Jeff V. Bolkan*
Production Editors: *Tina Wells, Lynda Gansel*
Production Coordinator: *Emily Reed*
Graphic Designer: *Signe Landin*
Developmental Editor: *Mike van Mantgem*
Copy Editor: *Kathy Hamman*
Cover Design, Book Design, and Production: *Sandy Kupsch*

Library of Congress Cataloging-in-Publication Data

Bass, William L., 1973–
From inspiration to red carpet : host your own student film festival / William L. Bass,
  Christian Goodrich, Kim Lindskog. — First edition.
    pages cm
  Includes bibliographical references.
  ISBN 978-1-56484-323-4
  1. Student activities—United States. 2. Students—United States. 3. Film festivals—
  United States. 4. Schools—Exercises and recreations—United States. 5. Motion pictures
  in education—United States.   I. Goodrich, Christian. II. Lindskog, Kim. III. Title.
  LB3607.B34 2013
  373.180973—dc23

                                                                      2012037372

First Edition
ISBN: 978-1-56484-323-4 (paperback)
ISBN: 978-1-56484-479-3 (e-book)
Printed in the United States of America

Cover Photographs: Maried Swapp

Inside Images: William Bass (Figures 5.1 and 5.2, p. 66; Figure 6.1, p. 74; and Figure 10.1, p. 143); Kaitlyn Mayse (Figure 6.2, p. 83); Victoria Arechiga (Figure 6.3, p. 83); Madeleine Sienkiewicz (Figure 6.4, p. 83); and Jennifer Young (Figure 8.1, p. 120)

ISTE® is a registered trademark of the International Society for Technology in Education.

About ISTE

The International Society for Technology in Education (ISTE) is the trusted source for professional development, knowledge generation, advocacy, and leadership for innovation. ISTE is the premier membership association for educators and education leaders engaged in improving teaching and learning by advancing the effective use of technology in PK–12 and teacher education.

Home to ISTE's annual conference and exposition and the widely adopted NETS, ISTE represents more than 100,000 professionals worldwide. We support our members with information, networking opportunities, and guidance as they face the challenge of transforming education. To find out more about these and other ISTE initiatives, visit our website at www.iste.org.

As part of our mission, ISTE Book Publishing works with experienced educators to develop and produce practical resources for classroom teachers, teacher educators, and technology leaders. Every manuscript we select for publication is carefully peer-reviewed and professionally edited. We value your feedback on this book and other ISTE products. Email us at books@iste.org.

International Society for Technology in Education
Washington, DC, Office:
    1710 Rhode Island Ave. NW, Suite 900, Washington, DC 20036-3132
Eugene, Oregon, Office:
    180 West 8th Ave., Suite 300, Eugene, OR 97401-2916
Order Desk: 1.800.336.5191
Order Fax: 1.541.302.3778
Customer Service: orders@iste.org
Book Publishing: books@iste.org
Book Sales and Marketing: booksmarketing@iste.org
Web: www.iste.org

About the Authors

 **William L. Bass** is a former middle and high school English teacher who now works with teachers as a technology integration specialist (TIS) in the Parkway School District and as an adjunct professor of educational technology for Missouri Baptist University. A speaker, writer, and professional developer, he focuses on systemic and sustainable integration of technology into classrooms at all grade levels. Bill holds a master of science degree in instructional technology from Southern Illinois University Edwardsville and a bachelor of science degree in English from Culver-Stockton College. He is copresident of the Educational Technology Association of Greater St. Louis, a Google Certified Teacher, and a past member of the National Council of Teachers of English Executive Committee.

 **Christian Goodrich** is a technology integration specialist for the Parkway School District in Missouri. A former high school math teacher and coach, Christian holds a bachelor of science degree in secondary mathematics education from the University of Missouri-Columbia and a master of arts in educational technology from Webster University. He is a presenter, professional developer, web designer, and technology enthusiast as well as a member of the International Society for Technology in Education and the Educational Technology Association of Greater St. Louis. Christian continually works to design, create, and implement unique, just-in-time solutions for all development applications.

 **Kim Lindskog** is a part of the Teaching, Learning and Accountability team as a technology integration specialist in the Parkway School District. Her appreciation of technology integration is based on empowering members of the school community to move from being occasional users to confident implementers of digital age teaching and learning. Kim holds a master of arts in teaching degree from Webster University and a bachelor of science in education degree from the University of Missouri. She taught mathematics and science for four years before becoming a facilitator in the Program for Exceptionally Gifted Students. Kim has also worked with the curricular framework of the International Baccalaureate Middle Years Programme.

Contributors

Amy Johnson
Peter Larson
Eric Wonsidler

Acknowledgments

We would like to acknowledge the following people and organizations for helping to make this project possible.

Ashley Deckelman
Drew McAllister
Susan Pinson
Maried Swapp
Tom Swoboda
Angie Weidinger
Jennifer Young

Arch Graphics
HEC-TV
Logan College of Chiropractic
Schillers Audio-Visual
SMART Technologies

Dedication

This book is dedicated to the teachers and students of the Parkway School District who gave us the inspiration to create a festival celebrating the work and achievements of students throughout the district.

Contents

FOREWORD xi

PREFACE xiii

INTRODUCTION
What Is a Film Festival? 1
    Our Film Festival 2
    A Brief History of Film Festivals 2
    What You'll Find in This Book 3

CHAPTER 1
Today's Students, Today's Media 7
    Today's Students 8
    Student Media as Language 13
    Traditional vs. Digital "Texts" 15

CHAPTER 2
Education through a Digital Lens 17
    Opportunities to Create 18
    Media Literacy 18
    Media Fluency 20
    Showcasing Student Talent 20
    Teacher Growth 22

CHAPTER 3
Festival Planning 23
    Festival Essentials 24
    Managing the Project 30
    Creating a Digital Venue 32
    In Summary: Digital Media 37

CHAPTER 4
Working with Teachers 39
    New Opportunities for Teaching and Learning 40
    Teacher Buy-In 40
    Essential Professional Development 41

Developing Technology Awareness 43

Mastering Resources 45

CHAPTER 5

Guidelines for Planning, Considerations for Equipment 47

Entry Guide Booklet 48

Equipment Quality 52

Video Quality 55

Sample Project Timelines 56

Additional Support Materials 64

Planning and Submission Checklist 64

Lighting and Audio Checklist 67

CHAPTER 6

Behind the Scenes 71

The Festival Blueprint 72

Securing the Venue 72

Honoring Student Work 73

Printing 75

Analyzing Films 75

Logistics 77

Marketing and PR 78

Technical and Web Support 80

Promoting the Festival 82

CHAPTER 7

Event Planners: Two Handy Checklists 85

At-a-Glance Planner 86

Two Event Planners, One Timeline 88

Event Planner 89

CHAPTER 8

Making Movies 103

Audience, Purpose, and Story 104

Preproduction: *The Story Begins* 104

Production: *The Story Continues* 114

Postproduction: *The Story Comes Alive* 116

Movie Reflections 123

CHAPTER **9**
Curriculum and Assessment 125
  ISTE's NETS Standards 126
  Framework for 21st-Century Learning 127
  Formative Assessments: Creating Video 128
  The Importance of Summative Assessment 135

CHAPTER **10**
On the Red Carpet 139
  Orchestrating the Event 140
  The Auditorium 140
  The Control Booth 141
  The Lobby 142

CHAPTER **11**
After the Lights Come Up 145
  Reflections and Feedback 146
  Other Realities 151

APPENDIX **A**
Online Resources 153

APPENDIX **B**
National Educational Technology Standards (NETS) 157
  NETS for Students (NETS•S) 158
  NETS for Teachers (NETS•T) 160
  NETS for Administrators (NETS•A) 163
  NETS for Coaches (NETS•C) 166

BIBLIOGRAPHY 171

Foreword

It is hard to describe the looks on the faces of our elementary school children as they walk down the red carpet at the Parkway Digital Film Festival. With their eyes open wide and a tinge of blush in their cheeks, they tend to scurry down the carpet amid the cheers and flashbulbs—a little embarrassed from all the attention. But the embarrassment really isn't embarrassment at all; rather, it is a rush of pride mixed with surprise and an overwhelming feeling of importance.

You want to talk about motivating students? This is a motivational experience unlike any other.

While the digital film festival is the culminating experience for many students, even more children are motivated not only by experiencing the film festival itself, but by frequent opportunities to use exciting video technologies as an avenue to express their learning. And it all begins in the classroom.

As an elementary school principal, it is clear to me that by integrating digital technology with best practices in teaching, we can see tremendous gains in academic achievement, student motivation, and parent support. Our Parkway teachers are using digital media tools to bring out the very best qualities of their students' abilities. When our Claymont Elementary School students see an example of digital storytelling and then find out that they will have the opportunity to create a similar project, they are instantly hooked as writers. Subsequently, they take the project's prewriting, writing, revising, and publishing tasks much more seriously than ordinary classroom work. As students are motivated to write with their true voices, each child's individuality comes through authentically in the final product. When students have an end goal of video publishing, their work is typically the best they can offer.

I take comfort, as a principal, when a lesson includes a visual component. We all know that most of today's students are visual learners, immersed in a culture of graphics and videos on screens both large and small. We have to find ways to bring visual elements into our educational practices—not only in teachers' delivery of instruction, but also in the tasks we ask students to complete. When students can represent their learning through videos, they are working in a familiar medium that will certainly only become more and more prevalent in their world.

Another advantage of using video in the classroom is that students can gain real and immediate feedback on their learning. When students can go back and watch themselves in a video project, they can accurately self-assess and then make adjustments for next time. As advancements in technology have simplified taking video into the classroom, this medium becomes an increasingly attractive tool for monitoring progress.

There are, of course, a few drawbacks to incorporating video as a tool in the classroom—most significantly, the time it takes to record and edit the final pieces. But we have found ways to utilize parent volunteers to help photograph student artwork, supervise recording centers, and guide students through the editing process. With just a little bit of training, parent volunteers can help with much of the tedious work so that teachers and students can spend more time on deeper thinking activities in the classroom. At the same time, our parents appreciate the opportunity to be involved with their children's learning and feel like they have made a real difference as partners in our school.

Speaking of parents—those who attend the Parkway Digital Film Festival and watch their children's productions on the big screen become instant advocates for the school and district. Attending an event like this lets parents know that their children's learning is a big deal to the district! Also, the Film Festival is a demonstration in innovation that parents crave. The positive public image that results from a district-wide film festival is of immeasurable value. Parents appreciate a school district that is teaching technological skills to help their children succeed in this ever-changing world. "Wow! We never had anything like this when I was a kid," is a frequent comment heard at the conclusion of the film festival.

And what about the students whose videos are not selected for the Parkway Digital Film Festival? Don't worry about them. They feel just as much pride and satisfaction when they see their digital pieces up on their teacher's SMART Board during the classroom film festival. Their classmates clap and cheer for them, and the popcorn and juice are just as rewarding as the red carpet walk. Thus, the overall benefits of using video as a classroom tool outweigh the draw-backs, particularly when parents become involved, helping projects such as this one contribute to their children's successful learning experiences.

Aaron Wills
Principal
Claymont Elementary School

Preface

In 2006, the Parkway School District (located in Chesterfield, Missouri, a suburb of St. Louis with around 18,000 K–12 students spread out over 28 campuses) established the Instructional Technology Department, a team of former teachers who would be responsible for helping teachers use technology tools in their curricular areas. We were looking for ways to create an environment where teachers and students would be willing to take chances and make the use of technology an integral part of instruction and learning. We were all teachers at various levels who were coming straight out of the classroom. Each of us had used video in different ways and had seen firsthand how students could make connections with content when they were able to create films as a part of their learning. As a group, we wanted to begin to incorporate video production into the culture of the district as a vehicle for getting more teachers and students to use technology in their classes.

I was a high school English teacher and had been holding mini-screenings of films that students had created as a part of my class. I thought that it might work on a larger scale, so I went to Tom Swoboda, instructional technology coordinator and head of our department, and posed the idea of a film festival to him. At that point, the Parkway Digital Film Festival was born. After an entire year of planning, we put on our first film festival in April 2008. The annual festival is now an important part of our schools' and district's culture.

Bill Bass
Senior author
Technology Integration Specialist, Parkway School District

What Is a Film Festival?

In our district, the festival has become part of the culture and something that both teachers and students look forward to each year. It unites the district through story and bridges grade levels to encompass and showcase the learning that goes on every day in our classrooms. It has proved to be a catalyst of innovation and has pushed teachers and students to be creators of digital content and savvy media consumers simply through their participation.

Our Film Festival

When we first introduced the idea of a film festival, immediate visions of glitz and glam sprang to the minds of the students sitting in front of us. Their eyes glazed over as they stared into space, imagining what it might be like to be a part of the "Hollywood experience"; from the beginning, they were in. Initially, the draw of fame and recognition motivated them, but soon, they found a different motivation, that of the stories they were planning to share. Since the early days of filmmaking, the idea of telling stories using images has fascinated the public, and these students were no different. Because the medium of film combines sight and sound, ideas that are found only in one's imagination can be brought to life when they are placed on the written page, enacted, and recorded on videotape.

The festival itself has grown and changed over the years since 2008, but a few of the original goals we made during that first year still hold true:

- We don't run it as a competition, but rather as a celebration of student achievement where we provide a venue to showcase student work for an authentic audience.

- We focus on curriculum and making the tie between video projects and academics.

- We provide ongoing support to students and teachers as they create their films.

- We make kids feel like rock stars.

A Brief History of Film Festivals

Since the first recorded film festival in Venice in 1932, artists have been searching for venues to share their stories, ideas, and techniques with others in the industry. As Kenneth Turan points out in his book, *Sundance to Sarajevo: Film Festivals and the World They Made*, the number of film festivals continues to grow worldwide, pointing to a variety of cultural trends. There are a host of active independent film-makers who "hunger for appreciative audiences, a need that dovetails nicely with audience members' yearning for alternatives to the standard Hollywood fare that dominates film screens not only in this country but also worldwide" (Turan, 2002, p. 7). These same principles hold true for student film festivals that are popping up in schools everywhere. In many cases, the students who sit in our classrooms have already been working with video in one form or another and would like to share their stories with a receptive audience, just as professional filmmakers and distributors are seeking an audience. Students push their movies out on YouTube channels and share them with their friends, but in few cases do they have the opportunity to showcase their stories to a guaranteed audience as part of a physical venue. The event itself becomes the culminating project and the platform for sharing stories and taking pride in their work.

So, what exactly is a film festival? Truly, each festival looks different, depending on its purpose, but on the outside, it's simply a showcase of films running in some kind of sequence over a set period of time and in a common location. On the inside, however, each film festival has a life of its own based on the motivation and planning that go into it. In some cases, the recognition of winning an award becomes the focus, while in others the celebration of the medium of film and the craft of telling a story take center stage. Regardless of these motivational elements, the electricity and excitement that come with a festival can be exhilarating for filmmakers and audiences alike.

In the pages that follow, we will walk through our history with the creation of a film festival in our district, outlining how and why we attempted it, as well as tips and tricks that might help other districts embark on the same type of project. In our district the festival has become part of the culture. It is something that teachers and students look forward to each year, uniting the district through story and bridging grade levels to encompass and showcase the learning that goes on every day in our classrooms. The festival is a catalyst of innovation and pushes teachers and students to be creators of digital content and savvy media consumers simply through their participation. It is our hope that other teachers will be inspired to plan digital film festivals and that this book will ease your journeys of celebrating student work.

What You'll Find in This Book

This book is written not only to give you the process and procedures for creating a film festival, but also to provide some reasoning behind our methods and procedures. We also explain why and how video can be a dynamic, rewarding tool in all classrooms.

In Chapter 1, Today's Students, Today's Media, we address the changes that have occurred in our culture due to the rapid expansion of technology and the accessibility that we now have to tools that allow anyone to create stories. This chapter also looks at our information usage patterns as we have moved from consuming the media that surrounds us to being participants in the creation of that media.

Chapter 2, Education through a Digital Lens, focuses on the role of media in education. In this chapter we specifically address the need for media literacy and fluency to be included in curricular offerings for students, as well as offer some examples of student projects that show how filmmaking and video can be incorporated into the classroom.

Chapter 3, Festival Planning, discusses our ideas for the film festival and how they evolved over time. This chapter provides an in-depth look at the planning process for the festival itself, including the need for a mission statement and our recognition of the importance of gaining support from our colleagues as partners and from members of the community as sponsors. Chapter 3 also describes the valuable lessons we learned about planning our festival from attending the AHA! Film Festival in Effingham, Illinois, and meeting with its organizers.

In our fourth chapter, Working with Teachers, we begin to get into the creation process and describe the support we offered to teachers as the film festival began to take shape. This included (and continues to include for subsequent festival years) professional development classes, resources, and continued instructional and technical support that have been crucial to the festival's success. Chapter 4 also highlights the new conversations that we were able to have with teachers around the use of video creation as a viable and worthwhile activity.

In Chapter 5, Guidelines for Planning, Considerations for Equipment, we describe some possible student projects, discuss some of the equipment we used to make the films, and outline the guidelines set for participation in the festival. By defining procedures and guidelines, we were better able to streamline the process and make the creation process more accessible to teachers and students.

As you might guess, a district film festival could be a logistical nightmare without having a solid plan in place. Chapter 6, Behind the Scenes, serves as a guide for much of the work that was done to create the festival. This chapter describes our instructional technology team's work on the films to create the final experience. Each team member's responsibilities are defined at the outset of the project. Also included in this chapter are discussions of the technical side of the system we created and used for the virtual festival, the submission process, and information management using a database.

Chapter 7, Event Planners: Two Handy Checklists, outlines, month by month, what we determined should be done or considered in a checklist format that identifies steps in the planning process.

While this book is not about making movies specifically, we would be remiss if we didn't address the process we used to help teachers and students through the creative process. Chapter 8, Making Movies, focuses on the creation process and walks readers through the preproduction, production, and postproduction cycles with tips and tricks for managing these types of projects in a classroom.

As is often the case, a question we are frequently asked when encouraging teachers to take the time to create videos with students is, "How do I assess this project?" Chapter 9, Curriculum and Assessment, addresses just that with formative and summative assessment strategies and rubrics to make filmmaking a feasible project for techie and non-techie teachers.

The culminating event for the film festival is the actual night when kids dress up, the red carpet is rolled out, and students are honored. Chapter 10, On the Red Carpet, brings everything together for the actual night of the event. We define each team member's tasks; as they all have fulfilled their responsibilities, participants can enjoy the evening without being aware of the painstaking work the team has done behind the scenes. This chapter outlines some considerations when planning and orchestrating the end result.

The final chapter, After the Lights Come Up, is a reflection on what was learned through the process of creating our film festival. During the planning and execution of the early festivals, not everything went smoothly. However, over the years, we have been able to adapt and create a better experience for the students and teachers in our district. In Chapter 11, we discuss how we have streamlined the process to honor more students and to make video a more integral part of our district's culture.

CHAPTER 1

Today's Students, Today's Media

Through a film festival, educators can honor student work in our digital age. Educators can help students make connections with the existing curriculum by giving them opportunities to move beyond the traditional learner role and apply their learning to the art and science of digital storytelling. Students are motivated by transferring their knowledge and understanding to the real world. Ultimately, a film festival inspires kids and gives them a venue for showcasing that inspiration.

Today's Students

Students today think in different ways from their counterparts a generation ago. Today's students process information differently. They've never known a world without technology and the Internet. Cell phones have been a part of everyday life for most of our students almost since they were born. The ways they access and work with information differ drastically from students who started school just fifteen years ago. Encyclopedias and phone books have been replaced by websites; specific facts about any topic can be accessed from mobile devices regardless of one's location. In a world with instant access, the connections young people make in today's culture can be more significant to themselves and to the world than ever before. A word "spoken" online can be heard and acted upon on the other side of the world. Teachers are no longer the sole purveyors of information. With a few mouse clicks, students can access the facts that composed the bulk of our curricula in the past. The 2010 National Educational Technology Plan (NETP), *Transforming American Education: Learning Powered by Technology*, recognizes the adaptations that students have found.

> Many students' lives today are filled with technology that gives them mobile access to information and resources 24/7, enables them to create multimedia content and share it with the world, and allows them to participate in online social networks where people from all over the world share ideas, collaborate, and learn new things. Outside school, students are free to pursue their passions in their own way and at their own pace. The opportunities are limitless, borderless, and instantaneous. (U.S. Department of Education, 2010, p. x)

No longer can we deny or ignore this trend in educational circles. Information has changed. Our world has changed. Through this change, each generation of students has been watching—watching struggles and watching successes. With these world-wide changes in communication, students respond to their surroundings in different ways, and our world, in turn, is changing in response to our students. These changes have presented great opportunities for students to share their stories with the world. Every single student who enters a classroom has a story to tell. Some students are anxious to share, while others feel trepidation, yet every story is a powerful commentary on that student's life and experiences. The opportunities to create and share have never been greater.

Traditionally, through lectures and textbooks, content was learned by students, and, depending on how well they were able to recall that information for an assessment, students received grades, compartmentalized that content, and the teacher moved on to deliver the content of the next unit. Until fairly recently, for most of their schooling, our students have been passive consumers of information. Their teachers told them everything they needed to know. By and large, students were not given the opportunity to derive their own meanings from information and to form their own connections.

Now, we are moving into an era of asking our students to do less consuming and more creating: creating new meanings and connections, new stories told in a variety of ways, new types of content shared with classmates that, in turn, become instructional resources for learning. Then, as students begin to create more of their own content, their consuming patterns begin to change. They begin to look at content in a different light. They seek out connections and begin to make efforts toward shaping and understanding their world rather than allowing the world to shape them.

One of the challenges of this newfound freedom to create content is trying to figure out where and how the culture of participation fits into the more traditional role of education. Worksheets, essays, and internal projects that never see light outside the four walls of a classroom are not as motivating as creating one's own content in a world where self-publishing and online video exist. It's no longer enough for student-created stories to be shared with a teacher or classmates because students expect their work to be posted for others to see and, possibly, to connect with and comment on.

Feedback on students' essays isn't measured only by the teacher's critiques and grades; it's measured in seconds and minutes until an RSS feed updates and students read what their peers and teacher have to say about their ideas. So, does that mean that there is no place for consumption? Absolutely not, it just looks different now. There's a balance that must be struck between creating and consuming as one informs and influences the other. Through the use of video, students can begin to see themselves as creators as well as consumers, and we teachers can begin to help students strike that balance in their own lives.

> I am a big fan of the Parkway Digital Film Festival because I can see how it sparks creativity and love of learning in my kids. They have been so excited to research, write, and work as part of a team. Using video has given them a way to showcase their ideas and learning.

Participating in the Film Festival itself has also been a meaningful and memorable experience for my children. They still have their "credentials" and posters from the events where their films were shown. I think the Film Festival really shows children that we value what they create.

Creating a digital film also teaches children valuable 21st-century skills that they are going to need to be successful. They plan, manage their time, communicate, as well as use technology. I know that this is an experience that has truly made a difference in the lives of my children.

Laura O'Grady, 2011, Parkway parent

Cultural Shifts

Currently, a cultural shift is taking place, fostered by the ease of access to new tools and equipment that makes documenting our stories technically simpler. As a part of this shift, we have the ability to stay connected nearly every moment of every day, changing the context in which stories can be and are being told. Current events are now being spread through social networks as well as through traditional media. Pictures are being uploaded, videos are being viewed, and text messages are being written at amazing rates. Yet these media, on which most adults rely, are largely ignored in the classroom because they do not fit into a traditional learning environment. The stories these pictures and videos communicate are being told in more customary ways, not necessarily because the messages are better, but often because traditional media are more comfortable for the adults who are responsible for student learning.

Modern classrooms no longer fit the iconic images that spring forth in the minds of educators. Rather, they are becoming dynamic learning spaces where students are connected to a wealth of resources and information. We are living in a time of change—a time where technology is changing the way stories are told, a time of global perspectives that have democratized the telling of our stories. We no longer need to rely solely on the traditional media of print, radio, and television; instead, we as individuals can contribute to the stories being told worldwide.

So, what does this mean for educators? It means we need to stretch ourselves so we can stretch our students. We may not live completely in their world, but we need to have an understanding of and an appreciation for the fact that their world is different from the one we grew up in, and we need to ask ourselves the question, "How should this difference change the way I teach?"

In 2008, Michael Wesch, associate professor of cultural anthropology at Kansas State University, made a presentation at the Library of Congress entitled "An Anthropological Introduction to YouTube" (www.youtube.com/watch?v=TPAO-lZ4_hU), in which he describes how YouTube and websites like it have changed the way we, as members of society, relate to each other. In his talk he suggests that "media is not just content, nor is it just the tools for communication. Media mediate human relationships" (2008). The relationships that are built online through the use of media are as important as the tools and the content. The Internet has been a disruptive force over who controls the message that that media conveys. So, as Wesch says, "When media change, human relationships change" (2008).

As we look at the landscape of education today, we recognize transformations in media that have changed the relationships among students and teachers. In this age of participation in information creation and delivery, students are changing how they approach schoolwork and how they interact with academic content. Our students are members of a participatory culture where creation is the norm and sharing is second nature.

According to a 2005 study conducted by Amanda Lenhart and Mary Madden and supported by the Pew Internet and American Life Project, over half of teens who go online "create content for the Internet. Among Internet-using teens, 57% (or 50% of *all* teens, roughly 12 million youth) are what might be called Content Creators" (p. 1). The study defines Content Creators as "online teens who have created or worked on a blog or web page, shared original creative content, or remixed content found online into a new creation" (Lenhart & Madden, p. 1).

This research indicates that with no training, relatively little in the way of resources, and without organized distribution methods, at least half of our students (and doubtless many more as of 2013) are creating and sharing media for friends and strangers alike. In the sheltered world of education, this is an uncomfortable place for adults who, as a whole, find solace in being consumers of world media rather than its creators.

In a report sponsored by the John D. and Catherine T. MacArthur Foundation, *Confronting the Challenges of Participatory Culture: Media Education for the 21st Century*, Henry Jenkins with coauthors Ravi Purushotma, Margaret Weigel, Katie Clinton, and Alice J. Robison (2006), state, "Participatory culture is emerging as the culture absorbs and responds to the explosion of new media technologies that make it possible for average consumers to archive, annotate, appropriate, and recirculate media content in powerful new ways" (p. 8).

Jenkins et al. define participatory culture as one with the following characteristics:

1. Relatively low barriers to artistic expression and civic engagement,

2. Strong support for creating and sharing one's creations with others,

3. Some type of informal mentorship whereby what is known by the most experienced is passed along to novices,

4. Members who believe that their contributions matter, and

5. Members who feel some degree of social connection with one another (at the least, they care what other people think about what they have created). (pp. 5–6)

In the real world, students consider themselves content creators. They are participating in the media revolution and are finding their voices online. They are writers, composers, videographers, and producers of real content, and they have a real audience. As Clay Shirkey (2008) states in his book, *Here Comes Everybody: The Power of Organizing Without Organizations*, "The future presented by the Internet is the mass amateurization of publishing and a switch from 'Why publish this?' to 'Why not?'" (p. 58). It's not until they come into the classroom that students have to ask if they are allowed to publish something that they created.

We are living in a historic moment where the media that is a part of our world is ever changing. Video and film have been around for decades, but incorporating video creation projects into the curriculum always seemed a little cumbersome and out of reach because of software and hardware demands. Gone are the days of dual VCR editing bays, where students had to pore over video for hours to edit and put their stories together. Instead, video that is taken on a cell phone can be edited right on the phone before it's uploaded to a site like YouTube. And then it can be shared with the world and viewed by others on their mobile devices.

More traditional hardware and software, like cameras and computers, are no longer vital for filming and sharing compelling stories. Students are creating more and more content and publishing it in a variety of ways. They don't need adults to do it for them. Instead of waiting for direction or help with a complicated system and a tape that can easily be erased, students are working in the digital world where storage is so prevalent that nondestructive editing is commonplace. Modern media are part of our students' language. As educators, we need to understand and include these components of communication as parts of our instruction.

In all curricular areas, effective communication is a vital component of students' work, but many times the communication skills that go along with that work are relegated to traditional media and techniques, thereby negating the legitimacy of formats that students consider to be "theirs." Video is now an integral part of everyday life due to the proliferation of webcams, camera phones, and other portable recorders. By ignoring this trend in the classroom setting, we only alienate students as they attempt to conform to outdated educational practices. Instead, we need to provide students more "relevant and personalized learning experiences … that mirror students' daily lives and the reality of their futures" (U.S. Department of Education, 2010, p. x).

Student Media as Language

Language is a function of society that we rely on as we navigate our lives. It is constantly being molded and manipulated as we search to make meaning of our surroundings and to communicate ideas, needs, and thoughts. As our language continues to develop, we have to ask what it means to be literate in today's world. Twenty years ago, being literate meant that one could read and write; that still holds true today, but now being a part of literate society entails so much more. The way we use language has changed, and with it our view of the world has changed. Increasingly, the medium of video is becoming part of our global dialect.

We live in a visually saturated environment, awash in vibrant images and engaging videos of all kinds. They are part of our culture and part of the language we speak in our daily lives. Thus, it is crucial that we teach with a variety of forms of media to model the use of video as an extension of our language in today's classrooms. Due to the visual and auditory nature of video, a wide variety of learners can benefit from viewing videos, but their use must not be limited to watching. Videos and multimedia can prompt conversations and initiate ideas from connections that are made between viewers and creator. Viewers can then become creators and respond through their own videos to the original creator—bringing more people into the conversation by using video as a language in its own right.

In a 2002 study entitled *A Report on the Effect of the Unitedstreaming Application on Educational Performance*, researchers surmised that one of the primary reasons multimedia and technology are effective in the classroom is that they "change the nature of interaction in ways that help students learn" (Boster, Meyer, Roberto, & Inge, 2002, p. 58). The language of media becomes part of that interaction and provides context, explanation, and understanding, thereby expanding the connections that students can make between concepts and their own lives.

"How does writing about problems help me to solve them?" This is the essential question that drove instruction and meaning making within our Writing Nonfiction unit in eighth grade Communication Arts class. Through inquiry-based explorations of social issues, students identified problems that resonated with them in some capacity. After identifying a topic, it was up to each student to determine their audience and purpose for researching and writing in order to create the greatest impact for the work. However, every teacher knows that the following question is inevitable from at least 10 students: "How will doing this help me in my life?"

This project was far more about helping students realize the power of being purposeful with their passionate messages of change and expanding these lessons into their lives than containing their thinking inside of the classroom walls and stamping on letter grades. To make this goal a reality in the ever-changing world in which we live, it is imperative that we help students learn how to use technology to get their voices heard in productive ways.

Technology became the vehicle for one of my students to deliver her message to her audience. Sara decided that her purpose for researching endangered animals was to persuade people to "do something." Her point was that no matter where people live in the world, there are animals that need their help. Sara decided that her audience would be her peers and adults who could help. She realized that she would not be able to do that with the articles she wrote and picture collages alone.

In response, Sara and I partnered with Bill Bass, who brought in his video equipment and taught Sara how to create a film using the images and words she had already completed. Bill gave Sara creative autonomy, and the owner-ship of the film was hers. In the end, Sara's purpose stayed the same, but her audience grew from our class to hundreds of students and adults at the Digital Film Festival. Not only did Sara's level of engagement with her class-room learning skyrocket, but she became empowered by seeing and believing that she truly can use her writing to work toward solving problems in her world. Sara gained 21st-century skills to take her writing and her learning to a whole new level, which will inevitably impact her learning in and out of the classroom from this point on.

Nikki Posloski, 2011, Teacher, Northeast Middle School

Traditional vs. Digital "Texts"

Digital tools for communication are changing daily, and keeping up is simply impossible. Yet there are constants that make the communication process possible. In an article entitled "Orchestrating the Media Collage," Jason Ohler states that we need to "value writing and reading now more than ever" (2009, subheading Eight Guidelines for Teachers). The abilities to read and write are not lost in the digital world. The organization, creativity, and fluency required in digital communication are just as important as they ever have been. Students who are navigating digital spaces and creating digital texts are working through the same processes they use when writing an essay or telling a story. The end result of a digital text may look a little different from traditional text, but it is still as important as it ever has been to be able to tell the story effectively.

When we look at the process of creating videos, it's apparent that video production mimics the writing process in many ways. The same could be said for blog entries and photo stories that students create. It's the process of creating that lends itself to organizing one's thoughts and ideas into legible (or viewable) form and brings that story to a greater audience.

As educators, it's important to understand the creative process and help students to work through and learn from it. We cannot assume that even though the digital world is "their media," we don't need to have a part in the construction of the knowledge that goes on there. Just because students know the technical skills of writing and creating letters, that doesn't mean that they naturally understand the craft. By the same token, simply giving a student a camera does not make her a photographer. Is it important that we teachers know what buttons to push to film or edit the video? Maybe not. Maybe it's enough to understand the process and to guide students through creating. This, of course, does not mean that we leave students to their own devices to create haphazardly; experience also plays a role. We need to have created a project ourselves to experience the actual process. We can give student insights to help them make connections to content. The teachers who incorporate video into their classrooms are facilitators and guides who help students to troubleshoot; these teachers learn from and with their students. The work they do together is where the real learning occurs. The process of organizing and creating becomes the focus of day-to-day learning, while the final project reflects edited portions of that greater experience.

CHAPTER 2

Education through a Digital Lens

We created our festival simply to begin expanding the use of digital video throughout our district. As with many projects of this nature, we had some unexpected results that began to give us more clarity about why this type of project might be beneficial to the students in our district. As films were created and stories told, the film festival became a platform for student voices to permeate our community. Our students began to recognize that this was an opportunity for them to make a statement, to say something through their work.

Opportunities to Create

Providing opportunities for students to create is one of the staples of sound educational practice. It allows for students to experience their learning in different ways and gives them the opportunity to show concept mastery beyond a simple regurgitation of information on a standard test. However, digital tools have changed many of the ways that students approach such creation. In so many instances, students are turning to digital video to express themselves and their learning, giving teachers the opening to introduce media literacy components into their classrooms and to discuss the messages that students are constantly being bombarded with in an organized manner and in an academic setting. Framing that with the 21st-century skills that educators are currently exploring, teachers must begin to think about changing their methods of approaching student creation. No longer is it sufficient to teach in an isolated environment concerned only with a single content area. The ever-changing world no longer allows that luxury.

Media Literacy

In his book *Free Culture: The Nature and Future of Creativity*, Lawrence Lessig defines media literacy through the eyes of Dave Yanofsky, the executive director of Just Think! Yanofsky says that "media literacy is the ability … to understand, analyze, and deconstruct media images. Its aim is to make [kids] literate about the way media works, the way it's constructed, the way it's delivered, and the way people access it" (Lessig, 2005, p. 36). While teaching media literacy wasn't our initial goal for the film festival project, we have found that some media literacy skills are coincidentally being learned and taught in the creation process. As consumers of vast amounts of media surrounding them, most students haven't given a second thought to how those messages and stories were created. We've taken them for granted as a part of our culture, but often these topics haven't been talked about by more than a few teachers. A film festival can bring these important pieces of the media puzzle to students' and teachers' attention and can become a vehicle for starting conversations about how media affect us.

- **How media work.** By bringing video projects into the classroom, students can begin to take a look at the world around them with a different eye. The act of talking about and addressing the message that video can bring to a subject changes an individual's relationship with that subject. Many students report that they don't watch TV or movies the same way any longer. They have begun to look at these forms of media with the critical eyes of creators.

- **How media are constructed.** By and large, one of the biggest benefits to creating videos with students is that they take on the various roles of the project in authentic ways. By becoming creators of content, they learn technical skills that will serve them well in their futures. Not only do they learn specific software programs, but, more importantly, they learn story-telling and editing skills far beyond those of the normal word-processing and presentation programs to which students and teachers are accustomed. Creating videos lets them peek into a world where they can tell stories and communicate in ways that the typical text assignment does not require or encourage.

- **How media are delivered.** The Internet has obviously changed how media are delivered, and that change is reflected in the conversations that students and teachers have about how to gain an audience for their creations. While their films are definitely created for the big screen, large segments of the audience for these films are actually online. This presents opportunities for looking at online video in a different light, promoting conversations about how online video is different from longer form productions and helping to see that media aren't one size fits all; rather, modes of delivery are dependent on their audience, purpose, and publishing platform.

- **How media are accessed.** Just as the delivery of media has been impacted, the accessibility of media has changed. Using the Internet as a publishing platform, where videos can be watched on cell phones, changes the nature of how people interact with that content. Additionally, the ability to promote pertinent information about time and place has a profound impact on who receives that information and how they get it. For more information about the digital venue that we have created for our festival, see Chapter 3.

Though not in our original plan, these media literacy topics have become important pieces in conversations among teachers and students by the very nature of their work with digital media. While we lack hard data on how many teachers have begun to address media literacy topics directly in their classrooms, we have observed that teachers are beginning to recognize the integral nature of media as a part of their lessons and a part of the creation process.

Media Fluency

One of the ways we have begun introducing the topic of media literacy is to take the approach that Ian Jukes, Ted McCain, and Lee Crockett have taken in their book *Understanding the Digital Generation* (2010). They define some of these new conversations and skills as *fluencies* and classify them into six different categories. Referring to these topics as *fluencies* as opposed to *literacies* seems to make them more accessible to teachers. One of the fluencies found in the book is that of "media fluency," defined as "the ability to look analytically at the communication media to interpret the real message, determine how the chosen media is being used to shape thinking, and evaluate the efficacy of the message, and … the ability to create and publish original digital products, matching the media to the intended message by determining the most appropriate and effective media for that message" (p. 66). By using this kind of definition, we are able to better convey the need for teachers to introduce digital media projects by analyzing examples, techniques, and strategies as they begin projects with students. Additionally, using fluency as our starting point, the concept becomes more accessible to teachers and students of subject areas outside of communication arts, where literacy is typically addressed.

These conversations, while prompted by a film festival, have not stopped there. The ideas behind digital media creation have begun to permeate the district and have made profound impacts on students. In another of the fluencies outlined by Jukes, McCain, and Crockett, they state that "creative fluency extends beyond visual creative skills to using the imagination to create stories" (2010, p. 66). By bringing the combination of these (as well as the other fluencies) to the attention of students and teachers alike, changes begin to occur in the ways teaching and learning occur. While these changes may not directly result in movies for the film festival, the practice behind them enhances classroom interactions in ways that were unexpected.

Showcasing Student Talent

From the very beginning, we wanted to create a festival that would showcase and celebrate the talents of students in our district. So often schools are islands of learning isolated from the community. Sure, there are awards nights, concerts, parent-teacher conferences, and open houses, but each of those individual events typically highlights a selection of students from a particular building, curricular area, or activity. Rarely does an event manage to incorporate students from multiple buildings, grade levels, and content areas in one place at one time. The film festival gives students the opportunity to employ their knowledge and skills in a medium not often used in traditional classrooms. It allows them to solve problems, craft ideas, and share their talents with a wider audience, while focusing on the objectives and curricular needs defined by their teachers. In some cases, students' work on the festival has even shaped their future career and educational choices.

Many students choose to tell stories through their films. One such student is Jasmine Brown, a high school senior who was taking a multimedia class. Instead of focusing only on the techniques that she was learning in the classroom, she put together a story of a young African American woman who was exploring her race. In "Black Silence" (viewable at www.pkwy.k12.mo.us/pdmedia/?uuid=DEFA2A45-1CC4-EACA-CE0D08740B8141E4), Brown used her knowledge of filmmaking and storytelling to make a compelling film (Parkway Digital, 2010a) that not only helped her think about her own race, but also brings a message of peace to her viewers, advocating acceptance, understanding, and knowledge.

A group of middle school students created a film entitled "Cyberbullying" (Parkway Digital, 2009). Meant to bring awareness and preventive strategies to classmates, this film uses skits and humor to bring attention to the growing problem of cyberbullying at the middle school level. Instead of being asked to write a traditional paper, these students were given the opportunity to research online safety and, through their video, to offer tips on combatting cyberbullying, such as telling a trusted adult about bullying incidents, never erasing messages from bullies, and never agreeing to meet someone known only from the Internet. Before the project, these students didn't realize how big an issue cyberbullying was, but when they learned, they wanted to share their knowledge with classmates. "Cyberbullying" can be seen at www.pkwy.k12.mo.us/pdmedia/?uuid=310.

The youngest students in the district also created films. In "Green Eggs & Ham" (Parkway Digital, 2010b), a kindergarten class examined, documented, and sequenced the process of making green scrambled eggs. They took their own pictures; mixed, cooked, and ate their own eggs; and created and narrated the story to go along with the process to make their film for the festival. Through this activity, students had the opportunity to analyze a process and share their work with others. "Green Eggs & Ham" can be seen at www.pkwy.k12.mo.us/pdmedia/?uuid=E3B1C0D4-1CC4-EACA-CEA86EB40FA16376.

These films represent a variety of types that have been entered over the years, and all of them have two things in common: they are completely student produced, and they bring all students together. During the festival, they cheer for each other on the red carpet, support each other in the auditorium, and look forward to the films so they can recap them the next day in class. The film festival gives students opportunities that they don't typically find in traditional classrooms and brings forth hidden interests and talents among students of all ages.

Teacher Growth

A powerful outcome of hosting a festival can be that of teacher involvement and stretching classroom practices. A film festival gives teachers a reason to channel their creativity, a quality that teachers, by their very natures, possess. Over the four years that we have hosted our festival, teachers' interest has grown each year, and the numbers of students involved and submissions have increased as well. While the numbers reflect levels of participation, significant growth has occurred through conversations among students and their teachers. Conversations about filmmaking and storytelling using digital tools have opened up critical dialogues about choices that creators make when telling stories and how those choices can influence viewers. Questions have emerged around storytelling practices and creation techniques that are far beyond grade-level expectations that typically dominate the classroom.

By providing a venue to highlight the work being done in their classes, teachers who had never shown an interest in using video were taking notes and finding the courage to step out of their comfort zone and try it themselves. While the fluencies discussed above point to something greater, the impact of bringing a film festival to the district has dramatically changed the way some of our teachers approach technology integration and digital media creation. Instead of being something relegated to a few teachers who have a knack for making films and understanding the filmmaking process, many who had never delved into digital media are now encouraging their students to create videos and offering them opportunities to walk down the red carpet.

CHAPTER **3**

Festival Planning

As the goals and vision begin to take shape, one of the biggest factors to be determined is the scope of the project. Will your festival take place in a classroom or building? Or is it bigger than that? For the purposes of this book, our focus is on a district-wide, multi–grade level type of festival. However, everything that we discuss here can be scaled up or down as needed.

Festival Essentials

Planning and hosting a film festival can be an overwhelming experience. But careful planning that breaks down this large project into discrete, manageable components will solve logistical problems, help to focus teacher and student work, and create an atmosphere of excitement. The result will be a rewarding event that will set the film festival apart from other school activities.

Create a Mission Statement

To get started, begin by planning at the end. Determine what the final event will look like. This creates a vision of success. Then, as the plans and project progress, create goals and make every attempt to stay true to those goals throughout the process. Thinking about and answering key questions will help focus your mission statement. By asking ourselves three key questions (see page 25), we created our own official mission and goals.

Mission Statement

The Parkway Digital Film Festival highlights and showcases digital projects created by Parkway students in grades K–12. Using the knowledge and skills acquired in school, students have made connections to the curriculum and applied their learning to the art and science of digital storytelling, enabling them to be practitioners in the real world.

- Reading comprehension, writing, research, and math skills are developed and strengthened; students utilize technology tools to create their own media to communicate and to interpret their ideas.

- Students increase their abilities to plan, analyze, and interpret results.

- Cooperative learning and leadership flourish where student media is encouraged.

- State and national educational standards are met and surpassed in the exciting atmosphere of creativity cultivated through the use of student media projects.

Three key questions to consider include the following:

1. What's in it for the students?

2. What kinds of things will be learned as a result of the festival?

3. How does this festival support the goals of the school or district?

Secure Financing

Someone once stated that there are no free lunches in life. Likewise, there are no free film festivals. There are costs involved with producing an event such as this, and finding funding in a school budget can be difficult. A key to putting on and funding the Parkway Digital Film Festival has been the development of relationships with generous sponsors. We have created a win-win situation for the students of the district and the sponsors in our community.

No Films, No Festival

During the first year of the Parkway Digital Film Festival, our biggest goal was to simply have enough films and content to make it worth the effort we were putting in. Regardless of the size and scope of the festival, participation will always be a goal. If there are no films, there will be no festival. The goal of high student participation should be the guiding force and set the direction.

Questions to consider in regard to financing include the following:

1. What will it take to put on a film festival?

2. Where will we hold the festival?

3. How will we market the festival?

4. Besides a good grade on a project, what other incentives can we offer students?

These and other questions will be part of the vision. However, begin reaching out to community members to be financial sponsors and begin developing partnerships with administrators, teachers, students, and tech personnel who will help out as team and committee members. These partnerships in our district became our basis for being able to actually make it happen. We want to make it clear, however, that we could not have organized and produced the festival without the hard work and support of many of our colleagues, including the other specialists in our Instructional Technology Department, plus numerous administrators and teachers who helped us at every stage.

As we do not have an auditorium in our district that can seat over five hundred people that is equipped with the necessary audio/video requirements, we needed to look at other options. Additionally, we wanted to preserve the idea that our festival was highlighting the district and all students in the district. By finding a venue off school grounds, we were also sending the message that this event didn't belong to a specific school but that it was all inclusive and everyone was welcome. We kept our search within the district boundaries and called upon local universities to host us. In exchange for a reduced rate to rent the auditorium, we put the name of the university on all of our marketing information and invited all participants and their families to the event. This also serves as a way for the university to showcase its school and facilities to local patrons and future students.

Marketing tools, such as posters (created by our students), invitations, programs, and VIP badges for students, can be very costly. Once again we turned to our community and found a printing company that was willing to print all of our materials at a much reduced rate. For our part, we included that company's logo on all marketing information and offered the company a booth with a banner to be displayed in the atrium of the auditorium on the night of the festival.

Media coverage is a must for an event such as this. Early on when the film festival was only an idea, we were able to develop a relationship with the Higher Education Channel (www.hectv.org), a local area educational television station. Angie Weidinger, host and producer from the station, agreed to be our master of ceremonies. This station produced a series of three 30-minute documentaries to be shown on the air during the months following the festival. The media coverage not only gives the festival exposure, it provides students with an expanded audience for their work.

How do all of the necessities get paid for? In exchange for monetary donations, we make sure that sponsors are recognized on all marketing materials and on the festival's program. Sponsors' names are mentioned on the night of the festival. Additionally, sponsors are offered a table in the atrium where they may display signage and products.

Build the Team

As the Instructional Technology Department works to deliver sound instructional strategies and provides side-by-side guidance and support for teaching and learning in a technology-rich environment, the idea of launching the digital film festival was a natural fit. In our department, there are 10 technology integration specialists (TISs) who blanket the district and support teachers in each of the 28 buildings. Our hope in year one was simply to highlight and showcase digital projects that used the knowledge and skills students acquired in school.

In year two, we made the move to making tighter connections to the curriculum and applying more of the art and science of digital storytelling. However, the process of finding and building a strong support system when thinking about beginning a film festival, whether it is building-wide or district-wide, takes a lot of thought and time. Before brainstorming a list of people who need to be involved in the planning process, revisit the established goals so that any plans meet the scope and type of festival to be hosted. We decided that our festival would be district-wide and that it would be open to all students (K–12) and open to all curriculum areas in a noncompetitive forum. Only because we had already set a goal of honoring a large number of students and highlighting their digital work could we then begin enlisting help from others.

Creating and building a well-orchestrated team with the mentality of *all for one and one for all* was an essential piece in organizing the support needed to pull off a district-wide event. We had a core group, but even inside that group, everyone needed to have a complete understanding of the festival mission and vision in order for this to be successful. The festival was not a competition, but rather, a celebration of well-crafted digital projects. As the big picture emerged, festival responsibilities evolved in the areas of marketing and public relations, technical production and web support, event logistics, and essential professional development. This acknowledgment of responsibilities led to the discovery that all team members should own a piece of the festival based on their talents, which would lead to the complete buy-in needed.

Achieving film festival success relies on attention to details from the entire team (consisting of TISs working in groups with partners from across the district, a lead coordinator for the event, and a group leader at the district level). Whether the intention is to organize a festival at the school or district level, the team needs to have diverse skill sets and personalities that will help navigate through the complexities of creating a successful event that showcases original student work.

Some people to approach to partner with as possible team and committee members include the following:

- **Administrators.** To get buy-in from curricular leaders, there must be a strong connection between student learning and the goals of the festival. Principals, coordinators, and superintendents all can help raise awareness of the event as well as provide connections to community members.

- **Teachers.** As tech specialists, we know that the teachers in the district have the power to make or break the festival. We are not in the classroom with students every day, so our partnerships with teachers were crucial to having films produced and submitted to show. Enthusiastic teachers are great promoters of the festival.

- **Students.** The students who come into classrooms every day have a wealth of knowledge about technology and, many times, are eager to help with projects such as this. Enlisting students to create films and also to promote the festival are crucial parts of the project. After all, the festival itself is in their honor. Dedicated students are hard workers and can spread the word about the festival at the grassroots classroom level.

- **Technology personnel.** Depending on how student work will be highlighted—including digital venues—the Instructional Technology Department can be a great ally for technical support, marketing on the web, and creating connections to vendors and community members for sponsorship. We value highly the skilled people in our department as partners in this venture.

- **District/building committee members.** Committees are great ways to distribute information and find individuals who may be willing to help. For our festival, the district technology committee, which has teacher representatives from each building, was key to getting the word out about the festival and its purpose.

As we developed our team, we also knew that we would need to provide direction and expectations for the films that would be submitted. In order to support transfer of knowledge and allow students to direct their learning, one of our first tasks was to decide what guidelines would regulate the festival. In the beginning that first year, we had very few guidelines; it was more about seeing what the turnout of student work would be. After all, we had an auditorium to fill, and we needed to figure out what needed to be established, based on experiences that we did not yet have.

We decided that we needed to go beyond our district and look for other districts that might be involved in operating their own film festivals. We found our inspiration in a neighboring city. They had a different mission and scope than ours, but they helped us find a starting point for how we needed to accomplish our vision.

Look for Inspiration

We had our vision in place and a lot of ideas in mind when we had the opportunity to attend a school-sponsored film festival in a neighboring city. As we were learning about what a film festival might look like, we came across the AHA! Film Festival (www.effingham.k12.il.us/studentactivities/finearts/ahafilms/) held in Effingham, Illinois, just two hours away from us. We contacted the festival coordinators, Joe Fatheree and Craig Lindvahl, who welcomed us to their event, gave us full access to everyone involved the entire day, and answered all the questions we could ask. The trip became an information- and research-gathering expedition; we saw firsthand what we could look forward to experiencing on the day of our own event.

Experiencing the AHA! Film Festival in Effingham allowed us to see that a festival was doable and possible in our district. The organizers' willingness to answer our questions, to let us speak to everyone involved, and to watch their festival gave us a good model. This proved to be a huge benefit to us for our inaugural festival. We gleaned several new ideas and gained reassurance on some of our concerns by observing the details of what made their film festival such a success. In examining what would work and what would not work for us, we had to recognize the similarities and differences between what our two film festivals were trying to achieve.

One of the first things we noticed upon our arrival at the Effingham film festival was the similar philosophy of having the festival student centered. The students were front and center throughout the night, with little attention given to teachers or other adults who had played parts in making the whole night come together. There were a lot of students helping to make everything go smoothly, but it was easy to recognize the filmmakers because they had VIP badges hanging proudly from their necks. This became one of our favorite ideas. We knew that this would enhance the rock star emotion we were trying to evoke. As a part of our marketing, we had already asked a student from each high school in our district to design a poster to advertise the film festival. For us, it flowed naturally to use the posters as bases of the graphic design for the VIP badges, and the student-designed posters satisfied our goal of keeping as much of the film festival as possible created by students.

As we sat down in the Effingham auditorium, there was a buzz of excitement for these student filmmakers. The large auditorium was packed with students, parents, and community members who had bought tickets and were looking forward to enjoying the show. Then the lights dimmed, and audience members relaxed into their seats to be entertained by the stories on the big screen. And that's just what they were—stories. It was evident that these students had studied the technical aspects of filmmaking, from lighting, to framing, to perspective. But these aspects of filmmaking were not all that they demonstrated they had learned. Although these were important elements for the films, what we really noticed and appreciated were their individual abilities to tell a story. These stories had plots, tone, and evoked emotion. Their attention to the writing process was apparent, and we realized that this was something we needed to work on more with our teachers—creating digital stories, not just informational movies.

Driving home, enlightened by the evening, we couldn't stop talking about all that we had seen and what these observations meant for our festival. Observations and questions were rattled off with hardly a breath in between. What would be required technically to produce such a seamless show? How would we fit all our stories into the time we had allotted? How had they advertised to elicit community involvement? What would work in our community? We now realized we needed to give more thought to many essential details.

This trip inspired our thinking and became an important part of the journey of creating our festival. Until we saw the Effingham festival, we didn't even know what we didn't know. Many of the lessons learned by this other district we would have eventually figured out ourselves, but seeing their event really jump-started our thinking. They showed us possibilities and gave us a context for our own future reality. Watching their festival behind the scenes and from the audience helped us frame what our festival might actually look like instead of what we had only imagined it might look like.

Managing the Project

Our trip to Effingham definitely refined some of the thoughts we had about our own film festival, but it also made us realize that in order to accommodate our goals, we needed to create some structures to manage our growth and to continue to create a better experience from year to year. Keys for managing the festival project include the following:

- **Treat it as an ongoing project.** As outlined in our calendar of events, the film festival is a yearlong project that we must plan for accordingly. Throughout the year, we have tasks to complete that build up to the actual event.

- **Continue to build partnerships.** The partnerships that our team has created within the district must be revisited each year. As jobs change and new connections are made, the mission and vision of the festival must be refined and communicated to those new to the process. Each year we meet with all of our partners to reestablish those relationships and to advise them of any changes that will be made.

- **Cooperate as a team to advance the vision.** Each member of the team must take responsibility for different aspects of the festival. Accountability to those roles is crucial for success. Team members must take time to reflect upon and evaluate their responsibilities and how they are meeting them on a regular basis. With so many elements to the project, it takes the entire team's commitment to bring the event to fruition.

- **Evaluate and reflect on the event.** At the end of the festival, we each reflect on our roles and look for areas of improvement and focus for the next festival. Then we meet as a group to discuss our self-evaluations and ideas.

At the end of each year, the technology integration specialist (TIS) team puts together a plan for the upcoming year. Within our plan, one section treats the festival as a project that needs ongoing evaluation of how it is being managed. Considerable thought has to be devoted to how to govern the project. This means that our core group has to commit to the festival as a constantly evolving project, requiring us to continually check whether we are being true to our mission and vision. We discuss whether the guidelines written in our *Entry Guide Booklet* still fit the festival's purpose and whether all students are being honored in the best possible ways.

Our core TIS team creates many partnerships with individuals at all levels throughout the district to ensure that we accomplish what we set out to do with the festival. In making decisions, we have to continually assess where we are in relation to where we want to go. Our partners help us to consider important details that may have been difficult for us to see from our technological vantage points. The roles, experiences, and knowledge of all the people involved help guide us to make effective decisions while maintaining our focus.

Our roles within the TIS team require us to take responsibility for specific tasks on the checklists we've created; to clearly communicate our expectations to others to maximize everyone's talents, time, and attention to detail; and to make sure we share the same values about the scope and purpose of the festival. The experiences of all the partners (administrators, teachers, other tech personnel, and students) help us to clarify and shape the outlook of the festival from year to year, and the connections among all the people involved help define various roles. The knowledge and insights of the people involved shape our decision-making process, which, in turn, allows us to solve problems and make educated choices about future festival objectives. Additional benefits of group reflection include the following:

- Organizational learning creates an alliance to accomplish the project and ensures that all involved understand the mission and vision of the event.

- Continuous improvement in the processes, procedures, and culture of the event helps us to develop ideas for next year that will enhance the overall experience for students.

- Better estimates and scheduling evolve each year, based on actual data collected on numbers of filmmaker participants, films, students as members of committees and volunteers on event day, teachers, and parents involved.

- Effective team building allows all who are involved to acknowledge and clarify all concerns.

- Improved recognition and consideration of all team members and their contributions occurs when we pause and reflect on this year's accomplishments before proceeding to the problem-solving phase and planning of the next festival.

Creating a Digital Venue

In order to successfully complete a film festival, a method for video delivery and collection needs to be created, discovered, bought, or secured in some fashion. For any size film festival, these logistics need to be considered. We figured the best way to do this for our district was to have an online venue, such as a website, to give out information and to serve as a digital repository for the videos students were creating. Because we were dealing with digital student work that would potentially be available through the World Wide Web, the potential pitfalls increased exponentially. Disseminating the logistical information for the festival was the easy part.

Getting the Word Out, Digitally

Roll out of information begins as far as eight to ten months in advance of the festival. Logistical information regarding time and place, movie and submission guidelines, and general reminders are publicized to users via email and the web, among other avenues. Over time, video trailers and promotions are sent via email, and the web page is updated with links. The goal each year is to get teachers to start thinking about video integration ideas as well as previewing past videos. The newest approach to information delivery is via a mobile device. On much of the film festival literature, QR codes (they function much like UPC codes but look like small boxes made of pieces of narrow, black-and-white tiles) are used; these allow anyone with a camera-ready device to scan the code and be provided with a website specialized for mobile computing. Consequently, the future of some of the film festival materials may lie within a cellular phone or wireless tablet. The closer to festival time, the more specific the information becomes. A web page, depending on the size of the festival, is not crucial but can definitely assist in marketing. As long as a central physical location for written information is established, such as a bulletin board, student lounge, a specific teacher's room, or assistant principal's office, all interested participants and volunteers will always know where to go.

Collecting Videos

Because we used a website to get information out, we wanted to address the much more difficult tasks of collecting information and quickly acquiring student videos. We understood that if the submission process were difficult in any way, the number of entries would suffer. We looked at many "canned" options for our digital venue. The first was YouTube (www.youtube.com). Keep in mind that we started this process before many of the newest features in YouTube existed; we quickly found barriers to using the site. At that point, there was no way for us to have a central location for our videos, as channels had not yet been developed. The overall content on YouTube was largely unregulated, and there were no restrictions on copyright, ethical use, or moderation of user comments and ads. Even if all of this were solved, we still needed to convince the district and community that allowing YouTube in the district was a good idea. At the time of this writing, YouTube has changed many of these things, with copyright regulations, safe and educational filtering, and channels, as well as embeddable queues for viewing many videos in a linear fashion. In its current form, YouTube is a viable option for creating a festival.

Next, we looked at TeacherTube (www.teachertube.com). The issue here was cost. We wouldn't be able to do what we would like without a price tag attached, and we still didn't have the control that we really wanted in the district. Another possibility that we looked into that may suit specific needs is a program called PHPmotion (www.phpmotion.com). This program is a free, open-source YouTube clone. It runs on the Linux operating system, Apache webserver, MySQL database software, and PHP scripting language (LAMP)—all of which are free and open source. More currently, with the widespread adoption of the cloud, another excellent option for teachers is any one of the many cloud-based programs, such as Dropbox (www. dropbox.com); Box.com (www.box.com); or Amazon s3 (http://aws.amazon.com/s3). Some cloud services, however, may have a cost based upon the amount of storage needed. With each solution we found, some nagging issues kept coming up. In all instances, except PHPmotion, the videos would not sit on our servers, which meant the media could potentially end up belonging to third parties. If a cloud service is chosen as a place for student videos to be uploaded, be sure to check the Terms of Service for those sites. It was and is very important to us that our students' owner-ship rights remain with the students. For these reasons, we sought something better, and Parkway Digital was born.

Our Solution: Parkway Digital

With all the research completed, we decided that creating our own in-house system was the way to go. Parkway Digital (often shortened to Digital) was created by Christian Goodrich, a member of the Instructional Technology Department, in conjunction with one of the district's web programmers. This section of the book includes the technical specifications and processes for creating our online video platform. Because of our needs, we created a custom system that could be modified as needed; this section presents the basics of that system.

We began building on a Windows server running Adobe Coldfusion 8 for server-side scripting and Microsoft Access as the database handler. The basic interface came together quickly, but locating software to handle the server-side encoding was a chal-lenge. FFmpeg (a free, open-source video encoder) was initially implemented, but it was not robust enough for our needs. A software solution titled Flash Video MX SDK (MX), built by Moyea Software (www.flash-video-mx.com/flv_encoder_sdk), was purchased by the technology department to handle all encoding needs. This software has the capability to build an all-in-one YouTube-esque solution, but we only needed the encoding components. MX has the ability to be run from the server command line and through a COM interface, both of which we utilized. The next problem we encountered was with CODECs (coder/decoder). MX uses the codecs residing on the machine to process video. This requires extensive work and upkeep to the server as new codecs and compressions are released.

With all of the techie stuff in place, it became necessary to make Parkway Digital usage for teachers and students as seamless as possible. Digital was placed in the same house as our district website builder and online curriculum guide. Teachers can quickly find videos that link to their grade level or subject matter curriculum guides with a minimum of clicks and then seamlessly embed them into their own websites. To this end, a significant amount of time was put into the search features of Digital. The ability to search by school, teacher, curricular area, and grade level and to upload data added a layer of validity to the types of videos a teacher would find, based on whatever search criteria they specify. Once teachers find videos to use, they can add them to their favorites list for easy storage, embed them into a PowerPoint presentation or web page, or reference a video's link almost anywhere.

The concept of implementing an in-house solution is ideal. As different needs arise, such as features that expedite better searching, changes can be made to accommodate nearly every request. There is, however, a significant time requirement. The initial version of Parkway Digital evolved over the course of one school year, and it was largely coded by a single individual during downtime, so it is hard to accurately quantify the time spent. The redesign took significantly less time, around three months, but it had the same issues as the initial development, a single developer with no dedicated time. That being said, a custom-built system allows for instant change as the film festival evolves, as does the online management tool. As web trends change, the tool stays current. There is no need to wait for a provider to make changes and, conversely, no need to make a forced change based on others' needs. We are now using the second iteration of Digital, with the possibility of a third version as the district implements even better online security. Increased security is a particular concern as digital and social media continue to merge.

Teachers needed to be educated on what they could and could not do in terms of student information on the web. Students as young as five years old whose teachers created classroom videos for the festival could have their names and faces on the Internet. The NetSmartz website of the National Center for Missing & Exploited Children posts the following warnings for parents, educators, and law enforcement personnel on its opening page, under the heading Revealing Too Much:

Web 2.0 lets users share information online as easily as they download it. Unfortunately, people of all ages often reveal too much. … Predators are always looking to collect information about their child victims. This information may be used to identify, connect with, or manipulate children. … Cyberbullies take their targets' personal information and use it against them. They may copy and alter photos. … Scammers want to use children's personal information to manipulate them. Children … may be the targets of spam, telemarketers, and [email] scams. (www.netsmartz.org/revealingtoomuch)

A part of what the Instructional Technology Department does is to educate students and faculty on proper usage of the Internet, so the potential dangers to our students are at the forefront of our minds. We incorporated a mandatory check prior to movie uploads; it states that teachers must have filled out the district's consent form for student information and keep it on file. In addition, security measures have been implemented into Digital that allow teachers to decide whether the videos they upload are private to the teacher, private to the district, or public for all.

A second layer of security is also utilized within the submitted video. Each video that is submitted specifically for the film festival has a list of students attached to it, all updated and monitored within the Digital system. For a student's name to be added to the list, the teacher has the responsibility to check again for the student's consent form, as well as indicating, per that student's parents, whether we may publish the student's full name. Managing these names, especially when an entire class is involved, can be cumbersome. Therefore, a comma separated values (.csv) file can be created and uploaded to handle all students at once.

Digital Distribution

Putting videos online quickly became an essential piece of the film festival puzzle. Having the videos in digital form meant providing a large-scale authentic audience for the students of Parkway, or in other words, a virtual venue. It is important to remember that the Digital system is moderated by the teachers who sponsor and upload videos. Students do not have access to the upload process. The teachers, who respect parental permissions, dictate what is freely available. At first this meant that there was no public access to the videos uploaded to Digital. This problem was solved in two ways. First, an online gallery was created independently from Parkway Digital. All the videos that meet the criteria for the film festival that are tagged as film festival submissions and "public" populate this gallery. This means anybody who would like to view the videos may go to the online gallery by visiting the Parkway Digital Film Festival's website (www.pkwy.k12.mo.us/tis/filmfestival) and selecting the tab for Gallery or by going directly to the online Gallery (www.pkwy.k12.mo.us/tis/filmfestival/gallery.cfm).

In addition to making all students' videos available online, we created On-Demand Films kiosks for the event itself. These stations housed a web-based touch screen interface that allowed users to access, in real time, any video submitted to the festival that met festival requirements. The kiosks became an essential piece because only a fraction of the submitted videos could be shown on the big screen. To honor the most students in an efficient manner, a practical method of delivery needed to be provided. The kiosks became their own entertainment and recognition

> **TIP**
>
> Consult the Online Resources section at the end of this book for more information about key technology services and products that will support your film festival.

centers within the film festival. Parents, teachers, and students gathered around the kiosks, viewed videos, took pictures, and then proceeded to the theater for the show. The kiosks helped to solidify the night of the film festival as an all-encompassing event and not simply a one-dimensional venue to view only the student-created films selected for the big screen.

In Summary: Digital Media

The goal when this project began was to honor the voices of as many students as possible while utilizing digital media. Initially, we wanted to put all students' videos on the big screen. Thankfully, the Parkway Digital Film Festival has grown to be so much more. Through this unique event, student work can be viewed in a number of ways, each providing an authentic audience for the students, a task that only a few years ago would not have been possible. Student work can be viewed in the following ways:

- A physical venue for the film festival where the videos are shown on the big screen

- Real-time video kiosks at the film festival that contain search abilities

- A local area broadcast from the Higher Education Channel

- The utilization of a global platform available on the Internet to broadcast videos worldwide with the use of Parkway's Gallery venue

- Teachers' own websites using embeddable code

Many of these ways of viewing students' videos are only available because the Parkway School District made commitments to the development of and support for a district-wide film festival, a district-wide digital platform, digital learners, and the Instructional Technology Department. The digital venue is a remarkable and necessary piece of a successful film festival. For teachers, it provides an avenue for moving data and organizing logistics. For students, it has become an important part of their culture of instant access and instant broadcast. This facet allows a teacher, a school, or a district to connect with modern students where they are in a way that mirrors how they live.

CHAPTER 4

Working with Teachers

Teachers are the key to successful film festivals, and supporting them is of paramount importance. Creating video can be a daunting proposition for teachers who are unaccustomed to working with the technology that is required to tell digital stories. These teachers often voice their objections. But teachers who are taught how to use these technologies and who are presented with clear outcomes and assessments will not only embrace student filmmaking but also may become the strongest proponents of a film festival.

New Opportunities for Teaching and Learning

Hosting a film festival requires many different skills from all participants. But the actual success of the project rests on the quality of support teachers receive. After all, it is the teachers who work directly with student filmmakers on a daily basis and for the duration of the entire project.

One of the biggest impacts of the film festival is that it provides an opportunity for teachers to look at new ways to make their content relevant to the lives of their students. Students today document and explore their world through digital video. It is a mode of communication that allows them to be producers rather than just consumers of knowledge. Video promotes an educational transformation of the curriculum, so that teachers are now encouraged to go beyond their classrooms to create platforms where students can understand elements of the curriculum by utilizing 21st-century skills, such as employing their voices by collaborating on projects; sharing creations with authentic audiences; and crafting multimodal compositions that include images, sound, and digital video. Due to this switch in focus from teacher-centered to student-centered learning, we need to offer new development opportunities for our teachers.

Teacher Buy-In

One of the initial challenges facing our project was that of teacher buy-in. Using video as a teaching tool had been done sporadically throughout the district, usually relegated to secondary fine arts classes where students were studying media. Convincing teachers that it was worth their valuable class time to have students create video projects was not easy. However, we were able to get a core group of teachers who were part of our district technology committee to commit to creating films. As they talked to their colleagues about it, excitement spread, and we began to see an increase in interest among more teachers.

The two main complaints we received had to do with the two-minute time limit per video and the condition that no copyrighted material could be used in the films without written consent from the original creator. Many teachers thought our time limit should be extended, and when we were unwilling to alter this requirement, some chose not to participate. Luckily, plenty of others adhered to this, especially when we outlined our goal of honoring as many students as possible; extending the time limit would reduce the number of students involved. This appeased most of those who complained.

We will discuss copyright in more detail later in this book, but we wanted to use this opportunity at the outset of the project to educate teachers and students on intellectual property. While we still receive videos with copyrighted music in them, we view this as an opportunity to explain what digital citizenship is and how to discuss the responsible use of digital content. Through these discussions, teachers and students have begun to approach content differently inside and outside the classroom.

One of our biggest successes in gaining teacher buy-in was that we relieved them of the task of creating an audience for their students and gave them a ready-made publishing platform. All teachers want what's best for their students and want to give them learning experiences that they will remember after the last bell rings at the end of the year. The festival gave teachers opportunities to create and share in ways that they hadn't been able to in a school setting.

After three years of the film festival, teacher buy-in was no longer a concern. Teachers are motivated by their students' excitement throughout the creative process and by the recognition they receive from the community for their submissions. That first year the festival was still an unknown, and our team created it through sheer will. We no longer get questions about time limits; instead, we are drawn into conversations around production and how to get permission to use copyrighted materials. Now teachers view video projects as opportunities to expand their professional development and instructional practices.

Essential Professional Development

Professional development … goes beyond the term "training" with its implications of learning skills, and encompasses a definition that includes formal and informal means of helping teachers not only learn new skills but also develop new insights into pedagogy and their own practice, and explore new or advanced understandings of content and resources. [This] definition of professional development includes support for teachers as they encounter the challenges that come with putting into practice their evolving understandings about the use of technology to support inquiry-based learning.… Current technologies offer resources to meet these challenges and provide teachers with a cluster of supports that help them continue to grow in their professional skills, understandings, and interests. (Grant, 1996, para. 2)

Depending on the level and type of technology integration in a school or district, professional development for teachers will be an integral piece in making a film festival successful. In our case, the decision to organize a film festival was made in part to spur more learning opportunities for students in the area of visual literacy. Once we had the buy-in from teachers, we needed to be prepared to support them with hands-on professional development opportunities related to their curriculum areas. To meet teachers' needs, we wanted to cover a range of skills—from the basics of using video editing software, such as Movie Maker, Premiere Elements, and Web 2.0 tools; to the art and science of the digital storytelling process; to managing copyright-friendly resources. To respect teachers' time and learning styles, we continue to offer support to all district teachers in a variety of ways:

- Create a film festival entry guide to act as a resource when we couldn't be there with them, which includes pertinent URLs, PDF directions, and submission guidelines.

- Distribute short videos to advertise the festival and to provide tips on everything from getting started to submitting films.

- Offer face-to-face development opportunities in the forms of one-to-one conversations; small audience presentations (curricular, team, or grade level); building level meetings (faculty or technology committees); district level technology facilitation committees; courses open to all district teachers; and curriculum-specific, coordinator-sponsored workshops.

Two more variables need to be kept in mind when planning professional development in relation to a film festival. First, consider the timing when the leadership team will offer different types of development. It is helpful to establish a timeline to ensure that teachers will get the most benefit from every development session. Second, consider that development at the elementary level may look different from secondary-level development. For example, in elementary grades, many student projects use Pixie by Tech4Learning; therefore, they need to do voice recording with Audacity to incorporate the story into their photo essay. At the secondary level, projects may incorporate Movie Maker, so teachers may need background information on how to locate copyright-friendly resources, such as video, music, and graphics.

With these key factors in mind, we also need to have a general framework for constructing appropriate professional development that encompasses what the teacher's role is for student-centered learning activities. Our responsibilities are to inform, communicate, and collaborate on appropriate ways to meet the demands of the 21st century. These entail raising technology awareness, mastering resources, seeing new opportunities for teaching and learning, understanding classroom climate in relation to new technologies, and guiding curriculum integration.

Developing Technology Awareness

In order to support teachers and provide professional development that increases the use of technology in classrooms and encourages student understanding and engagement, we promote technology awareness through use of Grappling's Technology and Learning Spectrum (1995), located on Bernajean Porter Consulting's website, and the Parkway Technology Proficiencies for Grades K–8.

Grappling's Spectrum is an instructional framework that consists of three categories, technology literacy uses, adapting uses, and transforming uses, which provide ways to map out technology skills, instructional focus, and usage indicators. Each of the categories of the spectrum brings with it a number of conversation pieces that can serve as entry points when planning and reflecting on lessons.

The first portion of the spectrum, technology literacy, uses focuses on the technology and the skills that are needed to use it. We often refer to this as the how-to phase and are quick to point out that this does not represent a low phase of the spectrum. Rather, it's the point at which teachers are instructing students on how to use the software or hardware, telling them what to click on as opposed to application uses.

In the second portion of the spectrum, called adapting uses, teachers are using technology, but that's often where it ends. Student use is limited, and the activities are often simply translated from old practices to finding a new technology tool that will grab students' attention. We often refer to this portion of the spectrum as using technology as an event, as opposed to true integration into the curriculum.

In the final phase of the spectrum, transforming uses, technology is an integral part of the lesson; instructional goals could not be met without the use of technology. In this phase, instructional goals, practices, and activities often look very different because the selected technology is a vital piece of the puzzle. Providing teachers with the Grappling's Spectrum tool has given them a similar language to speak in conversations about how they use technology with their students. We refer to it as a sliding scale, so that in any given class period a teacher may encompass all three usage areas as a means of differentiation, depending on the goals of the lesson. Most important, this tool provides a nonjudgmental forum for discussions about instructional practices that exemplify technology integration. More information about Grappling's Technology and Learning Spectrum, as well as a graphic download (which entails a standard written request for permission to duplicate) can be found on Porter's website at www.bjpconsulting.com/spectrum.html.

Not only do we use the spectrum as a channel to talk with teachers about how technology can be integrated into their curriculum and at which category in the spectrum they are utilizing technology, but it also provides a discussion platform for decisions on course offerings. Many of the courses offered navigate among the three spectrum categories, allowing for exploration of technology-centered topics that involve learning hardware and software; implementing digital storytelling through direct instruction; and planning student-centered, constructive pedagogical learning tasks.

An example of a professional development course we created to incorporate the three categories within Grappling's Spectrum is Using Technology with Classroom Instruction that Works, based on the book written by Howard Pitler et al. (2007), which, in turn, is based on the nine instructional strategies from Robert Marzano's work. During this semester-long class, participants have to submit assignments and lesson plans that incorporate each one of the instructional strategies.

One instructional strategy that lends itself to digital storytelling and multimedia is nonlinguistic representation. According to Pitler, "Nonlinguistic representation enhances students' ability to use mental images to represent and elaborate on knowledge" (Pitler, Hubbell, Kuhn, & Malenoski, 2007, p. 86). How does this work with digital storytelling? Research indicates that multimedia has the strongest effect on student learning when the student is the creator. Although PowerPoint presentations and movies are great teaching aids and can lead to higher levels of student engagement, the most engaging learning comes from students' creating the presentation or movie themselves as a part of the learning process (Pitler et al., 2007). Because this course provides step-by-step directions on how to create digital stories in the classroom, many of the products created by students are submitted to our digital film festival. Teachers and students appreciate seeing their work being published around the district, on teacher web pages, and possibly being shown on big screens.

Another framework for developing awareness of technological tools and instructional practices is what we refer to as the Parkway Technology Proficiencies for Grades K–8 (www.pkwy.k12.mo.us/tis/index2.cfm?goToLocation=proficiencies.cfm). These "I can" statements lean heavily upon the work done by ISTE in its NETS for Students (NET•S; ISTE, 1998 and 2007; www.iste.org/standards/nets-for-students).

The statements created for Grades K–2, 3–5, and 6–8 are general ideas of what technology skills students in this grade range should possess. Students should be able to apply these skills in many curricular areas, supporting and enriching activities that meet curricular goals.

Digital Storytelling—What, Why, How? is another professional development course that we created to support Grappling's Spectrum and Technology Proficiencies. In this course, participants learn how to create and modify curriculum lessons to develop communication, research, collaboration, and curriculum connections. The members of this blended learning community make connections online and face-to-face to engage in the art and science of digital storytelling. The learning activities include reviewing the research on digital storytelling, exploring digital production tools, acquiring the necessary permissions and consent forms for students, learning about responsible use of copyrighted materials, examining sample lesson plans and rubrics, and reflecting on student-created examples. The student-created products that are shaped by lessons designed by participants also support the film festival by populating the event with sound examples of digital storytelling.

Mastering Resources

A big part of preparing teachers to use technology in the classroom involves the ability to access, utilize, and master available resources and tools. This includes the ability to decide which tools or resources will best accomplish the objectives and engage the students in the learning process. Evaluating resources prompts many conversations about employing a variety of strategies, including the following:

* Planning lessons with teachers that encourage them to consult their particular curriculum guides so that lessons are based on viable curriculum goals that honor the district's mission, vision, and learning principles. Planning also provides learning experiences that are aligned with state and national standards. Once this pattern is established, sound decisions can be made on how technology can enhance what is being taught.

* Learning the concepts of a cross section of applications that allow for easier understanding of other applications later. For example, for digital storytelling, consider Mixbook, Storybird, or Photo Story. All have a similar concept, but one might meet teachers' needs better than the others. For example, Mixbook will require a teacher account and Internet access, while Photo Story will be loaded locally on computers with no requirement for

special accounts. These details matter greatly as teachers work with students in different situations.

- Being familiar with questions that will impact digital projects: In what type of classroom environment (computer lab, shared laptop cart, or classroom pods) will students create their projects? Is there a minimum age requirement for using a particular application? Are tutorials needed for student use? How will the work be saved and published?

So that teachers have opportunities to try out these strategies, the courses we offer generally require participants to be inventive and to create or modify lessons that incorporate the new technology that is going to be used in their classrooms. This gives them a chance to gain perspective on what they want to do and how to organize it. Throughout the class, they also reflect on their lessons, collaborate with other teachers, and give feedback on how the lessons worked in their particular situation.

Working with students today involves creating more complex, multilayered compositions. Students are now navigating ways to insert images, sounds, video, and text into their assignments to express what they have learned. We aim to continually provide current research and best practice strategies that align with technology standards to support sound instructional practices. As our technology team designs professional development opportunities, we continue to focus on the following:

- Mastery of basic applications

- Understanding best practices while integrating technology

- Providing opportunities for shifting out of teachers' comfort zones through blended learning

- Learning to scaffold content, collaboration, and multimedia compositions

Supporting teachers is, by far, one of the most important tasks in the creation of a student film festival. Ultimately, without the willingness of teachers to step outside of their more traditional teaching approaches, we never would have been able to provide a space for students to extend their learning through the creation of videos. Whether we give hands-on, face-to-face technical support or discuss a theoretical basis for using video in the classroom, providing the tools and resources for teachers is one of the key ingredients to creating such an event.

CHAPTER 5

Guidelines for Planning, Considerations for Equipment

Planning and preparation with teachers begins in the areas of curriculum, project timelines, and equipment/digital resources. Planning properly will save all involved hours of frustration and time lost in postproduction editing. Just as a lesson is planned, these projects must be part of the plan. Start with the overall goal in mind—a successful film festival. Not all classroom video projects will fit the learning goals of a film festival.

In this chapter we outline the guidelines and timelines that we have successfully used at Parkway to help teachers guide student filmmakers.

Entry Guide Booklet

During the first year of this project, we distributed a basic outline of what we wanted to see at the festival, but we found that some of the videos that were submitted were lacking direction and curricular connections. If our goal was truly to include video production in the classroom as a vehicle for technology integration, we were going to have to provide additional guidance and support to teachers. Early in the second year of the festival we were able to refine our thoughts, based on our experiences, so we created an *Entry Guide Booklet* to distribute to teachers with all the appropriate information. Thanks to the International Student Media Festival (www.ismf.net), we were able to create a derivative of its guidelines.

Based on the international guidelines, we customized a booklet that contained our festival's mission and vision, submission requirements, and curricular expectations. Our *Entry Guide Booklet* is divided into five main components, plus venue information and maps. The components, Basic Entry Guidelines, Categories and Purpose, Content and Organization, Production Types, and Technical Quality, all play roles within the three stages of the filmmaking process. In addition to being a guide that gives us a framework when planning with teachers, this booklet helps us determine the point at which our expectations have been met in order to accept a submission as a featured film for the festival. The booklet is also a useful marketing and publicity item in our press kit for sponsors and media outlets.

Basic Entry Guidelines

The first section, Basic Entry Guidelines, has to do with the submission process. Details on entries, credits, uploading, deadlines, and time constraints are addressed here. We require that all entries are original student work and tied to a curricular area of study. The curricular tie lends itself to the idea of producing higher quality videos that show transformation of content acquired. Individual students, groups of students, classes, or clubs are welcome to submit videos to the festival as long as each submission has a teacher sponsor and is from the current school year.

Any visual or audio material that is not student produced must adhere to the Fair Use Guidelines for Educational Multimedia and to all copyright laws. Students must give credit to all producers of images, music, and information in the production.

If copyrighted media is used, copyright permission release forms and written permissions from each source must be presented to the Instructional Technology Department as a part of the submission process. The sponsoring teacher will verify that the credits at the end of the film reflect that the required permissions were granted.

Prior to a teacher uploading an entry to Parkway Digital, our district digital media platform, each student involved must have completed the Consent for Publication of Student Information form and returned it to be on file with the school. These releases are required before students may display videos for public consumption on the Parkway Digital website.

Due to the scope of our festival, we limit the number of films that may be submitted for a specific project. Teachers may choose no more than two videos from any one given unit of study or project to be uploaded as entries in the film festival. Teachers select these submissions at their discretion, based on project criteria. Teachers' selections are meant to be the first line of defense to limit the number of videos and to get the highest quality work. Teachers may upload and share all of their class videos in Parkway Digital, but they may only identify the two top videos as entries into the film festival. All films that are submitted must be two minutes or less, not including credits. Films entered in the public service announcement (PSA) category must be one minute or less, not including credits. By remaining adamant about the time limits for submissions, we are able to foster more concise and focused digital stories, keep the attention of the audience, simplify the uploading process, and showcase more students' videos.

> **TIP**
>
> Setting a reasonable time limit for videos is an important piece in managing the flow of the show. If films are too long, the audience will lose interest. If they're too short, participation will suffer because of the restrictions.

Categories and Purpose

The second section of the entry guide, Categories and Purpose, helps teachers and students decide what the reason is for the digital project in the preproduction phase and provides examples of those categories. Whether it is the teacher or the student who decides if a video will be instructional, informational, documentary, persuasive, or a story, the category provides a focal point for the scriptwriting and storyboarding process. With these categories, teachers can focus on a specific audience and purpose to meet their educational goals, while providing students the direction they need during the creation process.

In the elementary setting, we tend to see more stories because of the curriculum guide's units of study. Examples include comedies, dramas, pieces inspired by novels or short stories, and those based on student/family experiences. At the secondary level, where subjects are departmentalized, we see more content-driven videos. The instructional category goes beyond simply presenting facts and includes tutorials and teaching tools. However, if students want to present a factual view on a topic or issue, they select the information category so they can create a nonbiased newscast or biography. Students and teachers who are interested in conducting more in-depth research will choose the documentary category, allowing them to convey serious research information through the presentation of facts and to go beyond the scope of a typical news story.

A popular example from the persuasive/public announcement category is the movie trailer. Many students use this avenue to persuade us to read a particular book from the library. Public service announcements designed to change public opinion, actions, or feelings are also popular because they allow students a voice on a particular idea, concept, or organization. A common PSA topic at the elementary and middle school levels has been bullying. More often than not, these videos are shown to other classes as teachers talk about character and relationships with peers. Through their work, these students have created content that is helping others in their school community. The connections that they make through this process stick with them far longer than the single film festival event.

Content and Organization

Some other topics for discussion between students and teachers are originality, impact, purpose, organization, and continuity within the project. In the guidelines booklet, this all falls under the Content and Organization category. The acquisition of knowledge, the journey through the writing process, and the use of multimedia content transfers into an emotional connection and experience that meets the needs of the most diverse learners. When students create digital projects, one of the most important factors is that the project achieves the stated goals for a particular unit and includes evidence of transfer of knowledge and higher order thinking skills. But it doesn't end there. Other relevant factors in this category include emotional impact, creativity/originality, and continuity. The idea is to create a fresh, meaningful, and interesting insight into a well-paced, high interest story that demonstrates understanding of and adds meaning to the topic of the production.

Production Types

When planning a digital project, teachers need to ask themselves, What type of production matches the needs and skills of my students? Production Types include live action, animation, sequential stills, photographic video essay, and video podcast. Each has its place in meeting production goals. If a teacher is a novice at using the tools of digital storytelling, a place to start may be with digital still pictures and Microsoft Photo Story. This program allows teachers and students to create a simple video with pictures. Using photographs simplifies the production process in a couple of ways: it eliminates the complications of lighting and sufficient audio quality, and the program calculates the amount of footage needed to express the message. At this point the emphasis is on putting thought-provoking pictures together to tell a story, making them transition in an engaging way, and recording voices at appropriate levels. Remember that thoughtfully selected images arranged to tell a story make a more powerful impact than a lot of random images that fail to connect to the message.

Animation can be a great avenue for homing in on 21st-century skills by supporting computational thinking, problem solving, and design strategies. Illustrating or creating the illusion of movement through computer-aided or hand drawn pictures, clay models, or Legos can now be captured by easy-to-use video editing software or Web 2.0 tools, such as Pixton, GoAnimate, Sketchcast, Scratch, Storybird, or Xtranormal.

> **TIP**
>
> Some Web 2.0 tools require permissions for downloading and use off that site. Be sure to check the terms of service for any tool that might be used to create media to be shown in a public forum.

The live-action production type includes full motion productions that generally have on-screen talent in the form of actors, instructors, hosts, or narrators. A variety of learners are involved in the overall process of acting, editing, producing, and costume/scene designing. The number of choices and decisions that need to be made support the efforts to use higher order thinking skills as well as to require students to manage their time wisely. This is our most popular production type because it's a natural outlet for today's students; in many cases, they are already exploring and documenting their world using video.

Technical Quality

As a video is reviewed for selection as a featured film at the festival, attention is given to items relating to technical quality that affect viewers. Those items include images that are clear, lighting that is appropriate for the desired mood, onscreen text that is grammatically correct, use of visual effects that heighten emotion, and elements within the scene that are arranged in ways that are conducive to the message. Other considerations are given to audio normalization, vocal quality, and overall pace for the amount of information.

Equipment Quality

There are many variables to consider that can make or break students' final products as they work with video. Editing software and skills can only do so much with the raw video that is taken. Some of the items to be considered include the type of equipment available for capturing film and the finished video's audience as well as playback venue. For instance, a video that will only be played on a website can be of a lower quality than video that will eventually be put on a DVD. By outlining and addressing issues of equipment quality before production starts, the project will go far more smoothly.

Video seems to be incorporated into just about every device these days, from MP3 and MP4 players and phones, to high-end still cameras and beyond. Understanding the limitations that come with this proliferation of technology is especially important when it comes to incorporating video into the classroom. Not every device records video in the same way or to the same file type. WMV, MOV, AVI, and MPEG4 are some of the more common file types, but that list is in no way comprehensive. This is just a small sampling of the types of digital files that today's video devices create.

> **TIP**
>
> Converting video takes time. If it's necessary to convert the raw video to a type that is compatible with the available software, allow for that conversion time.

Some video cameras still record to a tape. What file type does the editing software handle? If a converter will be used at some point in the project, does it accept the file type being created, and can it convert it in a clean fashion? These are extremely important questions to ask before starting any project. Whichever device is chosen, it is wise to capture a quick clip or two with it and see if the editing or uploading tools are compatible with the video files. If not, searching online for a converter or using one of the converting websites that are available will have to be a step that's built into a project timeline.

One of the simplest tools out there for video capture is the small flash memory camera. These come in a wide variety of brands, such as Vado, Sanyo, and Kodak, but all are similar in nature and, because of their inexpensive price point and ease of use, are very attractive to schools. Some things to consider when using these types of devices are the following:

- The microphones located on these tend to be small and of a lower quality so sound may be an issue. Be sure to test this in an environment with similar conditions before letting students begin taping.

- The zoom range is very short, so taping must be done close to the subject matter if the story calls for close proximity to the actors.

- No antishake features are built into most of these camcorders, so a tripod is strongly suggested.

Another recording device is the hand-sized camcorder. Provided by a range of brands, including Sony, Canon, and Panasonic, these video-capture devices provide a greater level of control and quality than the smaller cameras listed above. Some characteristics of hand-sized camcorders to consider—compared with those of flash memory cameras—are the following:

- They capture video to a variety of media, including tape, flash memory, memory card, and DVD.

- The lenses on camcorders tend to be much larger than those of flash memory cameras and can adjust for larger variances in lighting conditions and motion, resulting in overall better picture quality.

- The camcorders' microphones are larger and more powerful, picking up sounds with greater clarity. Many even have microphone jacks where external microphones can be connected.

- Subject matter can be as close as one foot or as distant as across a field due to a higher level of zoom range and greater quality of capture. Remember though, the farther away the subject, the more difficult it will be for the microphone to pick up any speech.

- Manual controls often allow for customizing capture resolution, simulated effects, and focusing, as well as preset lighting or environmental optimization. If set up correctly, these all lead to higher quality video.

- Transferring captured video depends on the media used. Most of these cameras provide for the use of a USB or Firewire cable. With the tape, internal memory, and DVD models, this is the only way to get the video onto the computer, and it also takes time. Be sure to build in time to capture the video digitally if needed.

- The video captured with camcorders tends to be of higher quality and will look great on anything from the web to the big screen, depending on final production settings.

- Because of their high quality, the files camcorders create can be extremely large and may require more powerful editing software for postproduction and editing work.

The most prolific devices in many schools are not even provided by the schools but rather come into buildings every day with students in the form of a smartphone. Recent advances in camera technology allow for photos and video recording on these handheld devices that rival the video that most video cameras were recording just a few short years ago. Be aware that some phones have better cameras than others and each has its own advantages and disadvantages in terms of file management and video quality, but the considerations for where and when to record are still the same as with the previously mentioned, flash-based models.

Because of their flexibility, mobile devices are becoming easier to count on and use for full video production. Mobile devices such as the iPod Touch, the iPad, and Android or Windows tablets, have amazing cameras and have the ability to help students better tell their stories by editing the video right on the device using apps like iMovie, Viddy, or Splice for iOS and Clesh for Android.

Another option is a regular digital camera that has video recording capabilities built in. Typically, these offer point-and-shoot simplicity, and their quality of resolution is often sufficient to fill a large screen without significant pixilation or blurriness. Higher end cameras capable of shooting in full high definition (HD) are also a possibility but are rarely cost-effective for the average classroom. A class focused on video production, multimedia, or publications may have a few of these cameras, but they may require significant training to use.

Video Quality

The final audience and method of playback will play big roles in determining the type of device you decide to use to capture video. There is a dramatic difference between an online audience and a group of people viewing films in a large auditorium or theater. Image quality can always be lowered to meet the needs of playback, but it cannot be raised without adversely affecting the viewing experience, making the picture blurry and blocky. When you're unsure how the final product will be presented, always err on the side of higher quality. Editing cannot raise the quality either, so the initial capture should always take place at the highest level because editing and making changes will lower the video's quality. Captured video that looks great on a small screen may not look as good blown up on a large TV or movie screen.

Traditionally, quality of video and quality of equipment have gone hand in hand. As stated earlier, using a cell phone or smartphone to take video is incredibly easy and accessible; however, depending on the model, it may not provide the quality needed to show on a large screen. It's always important to test the equipment that will be used to record if possible so that there are no surprises later.

In conjunction with varying hardware options, software is needed to manipulate and edit the footage. There are many different software packages to use; some of them are even beginning to be developed for the web and mobile devices. Some free software, such as Microsoft Movie Maker or Apple iMovie, allow for transitions, titles, music, and so on but are limited in their advanced capabilities. Adobe Premiere, Apple Final Cut Pro, or Avid, along with other high-end software, provide limitless possibilities for video editing but also require increased time, an increased learning curve, and significant cost. When creating a video, filmmakers need to know how the final version will be viewed by the audience. Web video can be of lower quality than DVD video, and most viewers will not know the difference. Defining the specifications of the video is an important part of the planning process and can save hours of re-encoding of video into a format that will meet festival needs.

Sample Project Timelines

There is an artificial fear that in order to use digital video in the classroom it has to be a long and arduous process. Digital projects do not have to be complicated to be effective; but they do require organizing and sequencing. Students are more likely to meet their expectations and decide what is most important in a story if a timeline is designed and adhered to for each stage of the project. A number of variables affect the timeline: the students' grade level, availability of accessible hardware, students' software knowledge, and the number and types of human supporters available. What follows are some sample timelines for elementary and secondary students. They do not include the time needed to teach the concepts but instead focus on the film creation process.

Two sample project timelines follow: Elementary Book Trailer Project, which has a 14-day timeline, and Secondary Video Project, which has an 8-day timeline.

Project Logistics

Once objectives for the project have been decided, focus on the logistics of the project:

- Equipment: Cameras, tripods, microphones, computers, editing software, headphones, hard/flash drives

- Acquisition of resources: Pictures, sounds, music, and video

- Scanner for hand-drawn pictures

- Available hardware and software (for editing)

- Schedule for computer lab times, laptop cart check out

- Source Files: Where are the files going to be saved—on a network, flash drive, hard drive, or DVD?

- Support: Technology integration specialist (TIS), parents, teacher's assistant, student experts

Elementary Book Trailer Project

Video book trailers are short, less than two-minute videos that introduce a basic storyline, utilizing images, sound, and voice, designed for a particular audience. The purpose of the video book trailer is for students not only to demonstrate their understanding of the selected book, but also to convince others to read this book. Many teachers find that this project fits naturally into their persuasive unit of writing. Book trailers are great summative assessment pieces for students who have completed a whole-class, interactive, read-aloud book; a small group book-club book; or an independently selected book.

The timeline below outlines an abbreviated version of a possible sequence and explanation for an elementary book trailer video project in a communication arts classroom, using Photo Story, a free software package from Microsoft. Each scheduled day consists of a 60-minute block of time.

Day 1 1 Immersion

This is the time when the teacher will first introduce the book trailer idea. This is a great time for the teacher to show possible book trailer/movie trailer examples so that students can begin investigating essential questions for the unit. Some questions to pose to students could be the following:

- What are digital book trailers?
- What is the purpose of a book trailer?
- Who is my audience?
- What message am I trying to send them?

Day 2 2 Immersion Continues

The teacher continues to immerse the students in book or movie trailers. Students will continue to explore key components of good book trailers. Some possible questions to investigate could be the following:

- What do book/movie trailers have in common?
- What makes a book trailer good?
- How do images help tell about the story?
- How does adding music help tell the story?

Day 3 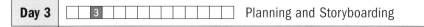 Planning and Storyboarding

Based on student discussions, essential questions, and curriculum standards, the teacher will create a scoring guide to help the students create a book trailer video. Day three is a great time to pass this out to students for project guidance. Students will constantly refer to this scoring guide throughout the book trailer process and use it for peer reviews later in the project. Referring to the scoring guide, students will begin storyboarding possible images for each slide of their video. This is an excellent opportunity to talk about where they can find images that are free to use. In this process they will make the following decisions:

- How many slides will I need to create for my show?
- What will my captions say?
- What kinds of images do I want on each of my slides that enhances my message?
- What kind of music am I looking for to help set the tone of my trailer?

Day 4  Storyboarding Revision and Polishing

Now that students have laid some groundwork, they will need to consider and make decisions based on answers to these questions:

- Where will I collect my images?
- What kind of equipment will I need to capture my images? (e.g., digital camera, scanner, Internet, other)
- What kinds of props will I need for my digital pictures (pics)?
- What locations will be needed when taking my digital pics?

During day 3 and day 4, the teacher will meet with each group or individual student for guidance or approval on storyboard ideas.

Over these three days, students will collect the necessary images and music for their trailer, referring to the scoring guide as needed. The teacher may need to teach these possible mini lessons:

- How to use a digital camera and save pictures into their student media folders

- How to scan in hand-drawn pictures and save them into their media folders

- How to find copyright-free images and music from the Internet and save files to their student media folders

- How to cite images and music from the Internet

Students will create their book trailers by importing all of their images and music into Photo Story.

The teacher may need to teach these possible mini lessons:

- How to import pictures into Photo Story

- How to add music

- How to add transitions

- How to add a title and citation page

- How to save the Photo Story project to their student project folders

- How to export the Photo Story project to a movie file

Day 11 Peer Review

In a small group, with a partner, or as a class show, students will use the Book Trailer scoring guide to peer review each other's book trailers to give feedback to classmates.

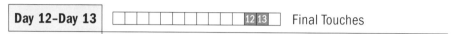

Day 12–Day 13 Final Touches

Students will make any last minute changes necessary (based on peer feedback) and finalize their book trailers. All projects will be exported into a movie file and saved into their student folders.

Day 14 Celebration

Students will exhibit their book trailer videos to classmates or to other classes and celebrate their hard work.

This timeline is just an example of the steps one teacher takes when she incorporates video book trailers into her class's work. Depending on the scope of the project, all of these elements can be altered as needed to meet curriculum goals and outcomes.

Secondary Video Project

This timeline outlines an abbreviated version of a possible sequence and timeline, created by middle school teacher Maria Flick for a secondary video project in a communication arts classroom with a block schedule of approximately 90 minutes. This timeline begins once the material that is being used to inspire the project is identified, studied, and researched.

Day 1  Project Introduction

Introduce the project options, based upon the categories and purpose identified in the *Entry Guide Booklet*.

- Introduce one category type at a time, using examples to illustrate structure of each format.
    - For example, with a PSA, multiple examples can be found on YouTube.com
    - Another persuasive example is a book trailer, there are multiple examples of movie trailers found on IMDB.com or youtube.com

Day 1 homework: Find other examples of both PSAs and movie trailers on their own, take notes on the strategies used to persuade and inform viewers.

Day 2  Planning and Storyboarding

Class discussion about homework, tricks they observed that were used in the examples they found on their own to persuade or inform viewers. Allow groups to get together and start the brainstorming process.

- Required to use the storyboards they created during their reading of the novel they read
- Required to use the same format to create a final proposal and storyboard to review with the teacher for approval

Day 3 Finalize Storyboard and Rehearse

Groups continue to polish storyboard and ideas; conference with teacher for approval. Storyboard must include locations in the building where filming will take place, the purpose of the location, and any props or resources needed from the teacher to complete the videotaping. Once approved, students start rehearsing.

Day 4 ☐☐☐ 4 ☐☐☐ Taping

Taping should begin. Define ahead of time the number of days/class periods allowed for filming. More time is not necessarily better! For a two-minute video, students do not need to create 40 minutes of raw footage. Typically, 15 minutes of raw video will do for a two-minute video. However, that time can vary dramatically depending on the number of takes students do of a single scene as well as the complexity of the story they wish to tell. Note that too much video will become overwhelming for them during editing. Since they have already created storyboards for their scenes, they should take notes on which scene worked best for them and which one they think they got right. Then they will be able to skip over the extra footage that they recorded and start with the one they feel good about.

- Allow time each day for students to watch the "dailies" of what they taped. They should take notes and make decisions about what still needs to be "shot" based on the day's successful filming.

Day 5 ☐☐☐ 5 ☐☐ Basic Editing

Students work in the computer lab.

- Instruct students on how to transfer video from camera to the student folders on the desktop. This one folder is where all work should be stored.

- Instruct students on basics of editing software, importing all video clips, and organizing the clips in the storyboard mode into a workable sequence.

- Encourage students to change "drivers" often so they all get a chance to use the software.

- Explain the importance of saving the correct way into their student folders and any other troubleshooting tips.

- Groups that catch on quickly or have more familiarity with the software will provide individual instruction to other students on how to make cuts/edits within the video clips.

Day 6   6   Adding Titles and Sound

Students work in the computer lab.

- Provide introduction to the students on advanced software features (transitions, special effects, and voiceovers).

- Students spend this day working on using these software features to edit their projects.

Day 7   7   Finishing up and Copyright

Students work in the computer lab.

- This can be day two of feature editing and title credits.

- Provide group instruction on how to incorporate sound into the video.

- Discuss copyright issues and responsibilities, including the need to ask for permission to use copyrighted material. Explain that many but not all sites on the Internet allow their materials to be used freely for educational purposes. Mention that for film festival videos, no copyrighted materials requiring written permission requests may be used. (The film festival website, www.pkwy.k12.mo.us/tis/filmfestival, contains lists of materials that may be used without seeking permissions.)

Day 8   8   Final Day of Editing

Students work in the computer lab.

- This day will be used in different ways for different groups depending on how far along they are.

- Final touches to the videos may be made, and final approval from teacher is given prior to rendering the final version of the movie to show to the entire class.

This timeline is just an example of the steps one teacher takes when she incorporates video production in her classroom. All of the videos using that time frame are typically live-action videos requiring filming time. Depending on the scope of the project, all of these elements can be altered as needed to meet the teacher's and the curriculum's goals.

Additional Support Materials

In addition to the *Entry Guide Booklet*, we created some additional support materials to assist teachers and students in the creation process. These include a Planning and Submission Checklist, allowing teachers to make sure that students are following guidelines and entering a quality video, and a Lighting and Audio Checklist, which students can refer to as they plan their locations in order to get high-quality video. These two documents became valuable in the planning process and were distributed via the film festival website and on demand as needed.

Planning and Submission Checklist

Use this checklist to help you plan for the making of your film and as a checklist of required items before you submit your film. Each checklist item has tips to assist you with your planning.

- ☐ **The film was created for a class.**

- ☐ **Finished film is 2 mins. or less** (PSA = 1 min. or less)—not including credits.

  - Rehearse before you begin filming.
  - Always take a 10-second test shot, and watch to make sure sound and lighting are good before continuing.
  - Use a tripod (lean against a wall as alternative).
  - 5+clip+5 (leave 5 seconds before and after each scene to allow for editing).
  - Use different angles when possible (to give different perspectives).
  - Avoid filming one person doing all of the talking.
  - Check backgrounds before filming to make sure that what you can see through the camera helps to tell your story.

Planning and Submission Checklist *(Continued)*

- Zooming and panning in or out should be done slowly and steadily.

- Save all project clips from your camera to your computer.

- Know the video format of your camera (MP4, MOD, MOV, AVI) and whether conversion will be necessary to use with your editing software.

☐ **No copyrighted material has been used.**

- Ask your teacher for a list of copyright-friendly resources that can be found on the Technology Integration Specialist (TIS) website.

☐ **Credits are included at the end the film.**

- Include the names of everyone involved in making the film.

- Cite all media used in creating your film.

☐ **Sound/Voices**—Speaking voices are clear and easy to understand.

- Consider wind and background noise in the area while filming.

- Do not read from paper (use cue cards).

- Use a microphone when possible to keep voices at desired volume (2 inches from mouth).

- Keep volume consistent between actors.

- Talk slowly, clearly, and with expression.

☐ **Lighting**—The image is clear, and the lighting is appropriate for the desired effect.

- Do not shoot directly into the sun.

- Do not film in partial light or shade; this creates shadows (e.g., under a tree).

- Use extra light inside (e.g., lamp without a shade).

- Light should always be in front of what is being filmed.

(Continued)

Planning and Submission Checklist | *(Continued)*

☐ **Text/Subtitles**—fonts are easy to read.

- Subtitles are required for all films not in the English language.
- Do not overlap text with detailed images or other text.
- Do not block anything important to the scene.
- Make sure it is on the screen long enough to be read (do not have too much text on the screen).
- Use contrasting colors.
- Use a large and easy-to-read font (fancy fonts are hard to read; don't use italics).
- Use correct spelling/grammar.

☐ **Pictures**—images are clear and of high quality.

- Make sure images are not pixelated.

Figure 5.1 Pixelated image

Figure 5.2 Non-pixelated image

- Use the largest image size possible (high resolution, 1024×768 pixels).

☐ **Effects and Transitions**—are used with purpose and not distracting.

- Transitions are used in a mindful way to create a smooth shot-to-shot flow within the story.
- Effects support appropriate emphasis in communicating the main idea.

Lighting and Audio Checklist

The mood, tone, and message are elements of your story that are influenced by lighting and audio quality. To save time editing, plan and prepare the recording environment. Likewise, take and preview a 10-second test shot to be sure the lighting and audio are of good quality before continuing to shoot.

Outdoor Filming

Lighting. It is important to get the lighting correct from the beginning as trying to correct this in the editing phase is very time-consuming and takes a lot of computer processing speed.

- [ ] **Sun position**—should be behind the camera operator.

- [ ] **Shadows**—can obscure subjects and their details, like faces, including hats with brims.

- [ ] **Moving**—from well-lit to shadowed areas will cause lighting problems.

- [ ] **Cloudy days**—are best for even lighting.

Audio/Sound. This is the most difficult aspect of the movie to do correctly, so pay particular attention to:

- [ ] **Volume**—Subjects need to speak loudly and face toward the camera if possible.

- [ ] **Proximity**—Talking subjects need to be close to the camera (within 10 ft.).

- [ ] **Background noises**—Avoid being near roads, playgrounds, AC units, and power tools.

- [ ] **Wind**—Avoid windy days at all costs; otherwise, use the windscreen setting when filming if the option is available in the camera's menu settings.

(Continued)

Lighting and Audio Checklist   *(Continued)*

Classroom Filming

Lighting. The camera makes adjustments for the amount of light available.

☐ **Location**—ceiling, lamps, windows. Try to be sure that the camera isn't directly facing one of these objects otherwise the subject that is being shot will be too dark.

☐ **Use extra light**—when available.

☐ **Panning across a window section**—can cause the camera to continually adjust to the varying available light.

Audio/Sound. Just as in outdoor filming, clearly recording the sound is the most difficult aspect of the movie to do correctly. Pay close attention to the following aspects of audio:

☐ **Microphone**

- Use an external microphone if possible.
- Keep the microphone at the same distance away from your mouth (approximately 2 inches) for the entire recording when using voiceovers on the computer.

☐ **Voice levels**—Keep all voices at the same level.

☐ **Noise inside the room**

- Avoid the beginning and end of class.
- Be aware of running AC/heating units/fans.
- Note the number of classmates in a room and how much sound they are creating—sneezing, typing, shuffling, etc.

☐ **Noise outside the room**

- Shut the door and put a sign on the it saying, "Please do not disturb."
- Be aware of outside sounds from an open window.

Lighting and Audio Checklist *(Continued)*

☐ **Room size**

- Small enclosed room—echo may be present due to hard floor.
- Large room—speak clearly and with more volume.

Additional Items to Consider
Audio Considerations

☐ Breathing/talking

☐ Walking

☐ Coughing, sniffles, etc.

☐ Swishing of clothes

Know Your Camera

☐ Lens zoom level (optical vs. digital)

☐ Microphone quality

☐ Available recording time

CHAPTER 6

Behind
the Scenes

As content starts being created by students for the film festival, there are a variety of logistics that must be addressed when planning for the big night. There are people to contact, a venue to secure, films to select, and many other details to prepare and organize. Where does one even begin?

The Festival Blueprint

In order that students and teachers are provided with the support they need, the planning and resulting activities must stay true to the festival's goals. For our festival, we want the production of the event itself to reflect the standards to which we hold our student filmmakers. The most visible of these support pieces is the place where the event itself will actually take place. Equally important are how student work is honored and presented, how the event is managed and publicized, and the types and uses of supporting technology that make the event itself a success.

Securing the Venue

An important first step in hosting a film festival is securing a venue for the event. It is important to us to host our film festival off district grounds so that it will not be associated with any one school or building but be considered a district-wide event. It is best to have one team member be the liaison for arranging and working with the venue. This person is responsible for scheduling for the date of the event, a rehearsal date, and any other visits to the venue that may be needed during the planning stages. The liaison will also need to inquire about and request any special equipment that the venue may be able to supply. Having a single contact point streamlines much of the communication that inevitably occurs. When choosing the event location, the most important consideration is number of seats. Again, this depends on the size of the event, but make plans so that there is enough space for families of students who have participated.

One way to get around this, as well as help defray some of the costs associated with the event, is to charge admission and have a ticketing system. We chose not to do this for two reasons: we wanted for this celebration to be as accessible as possible to all community members, and we found sponsors willing to fund it for us.

The atmosphere of a festival is important regardless of its size. One way to make it a special event is by renting a red carpet for students to walk down. Each student who has submitted a film to our festival has a chance to walk down the red carpet and have his or her name announced to family and friends as a part of the evening.

To further enhance the atmosphere of the evening, we try to get many students, district personnel, and community members involved. Having a communication checklist for contacting these outside parties is helpful.

Communication Checklist

- ☐ Solicit high school photography students to document the evening with photos from the red carpet to candid moments.

- ☐ Arrange for and collect high school student–created music to be played in the auditorium during intermission and in the lobby throughout the evening.

- ☐ Arrange for a high school jazz band to play in the lobby as students' names are announced and they walk on the red carpet for a grand entrance to the event.

- ☐ Communicate with the public relations department to ensure media coverage of the event.

- ☐ Arrange for an emcee to provide an introduction and closing to the show. The emcee's script will need to be written by a team member.

It will be important to develop a communication plan for all of your participants in the festival and tailor the message to the appropriate audiences. Teachers and students have similar informational needs around criteria for entering the festival, submission dates, and resources for creating movies while most other groups just need to know about the event itself. Find a balance between communication cycles so that no one group gets overwhelmed but that the information is out there and readily accessible. About six months before the festival, we suggest an initial announcement blitz meant to reach as much of the district as possible in both electronic (announcement video and website) and face-to-face (faculty meetings and other development) forums. After that initial run, a monthly reminder email with some additional resources and examples of previous movies is often enough to keep interest up. Two months before the submission date another communication blitz will help to get those last few submissions and get students interested.

Honoring Student Work

Due to the scope of our festival, we knew that we would be unable to highlight every film that was entered; we simply didn't have enough time. However, we also wanted to honor each student's work in some way. For the first two years, we created interactive booths in the lobby where student videos that were not featured on the big screen would play on a continuous loop for the duration of the evening.

Originally, we thought of these booths as kiosks consisting of a table with a computer hooked up to a HDTV where the films would loop throughout the evening. This was an important part of trying to keep the festival a celebration rather than a competition. These kiosks were effective, but the fact that the video was on a loop meant that once a video was played, it would not be played again for at least 40 minutes. It immediately became clear that we were not honoring those students very well, so we sought other solutions.

During our third year we changed our approach so that when students and families came to the booths, they could have a choice of which video they wanted to view. Using XML and Flash video files, we were able to create an interface that organized films by schools for easy access. Students and families no longer had to wait for the video to loop around again; they could watch any video that was submitted from the entire festival by simply selecting the school and the video. This approach has proved to be very successful, in that students can find their friends' videos and see what else was submitted from their school in one place. It truly changed the scope of the event in an unexpected way. Instead of the festival being solely focused around the featured films that were on the big screen, some of the focus moved to these On-Demand stations in the lobby that gave attendees a chance to watch selected videos (Figure 6.1).

Figure 6.1 On-Demand Film kiosk in festival lobby

Our final venue resides online. After each film festival, a gallery is created of all films submitted and can be accessed via the web. This virtual venue becomes an archive of past videos and continues to celebrate students for years to come.

Printing

Another piece to consider is the publishing of documents that will represent the film festival. Consistency in design and message is an important aspect to keep in mind. Having a team of creative desktop publishers has been very valuable for our festivals. This role also includes managing the graphics and photographs associated with the film festival, along with the production of a logo to represent the film festival. Below are some suggested publications for the event.

- Invitations to the event to be mailed or hand delivered to students and community members. A postcard design with the pertinent information on it works well.

- VIP badges to be distributed to student participants add to the atmosphere of the event. The badges also act as their tickets to walk the red carpet.

- Certificates of participation to be distributed to students after the film festival.

- Event programs that convey the vision of the film festival along with a sequential listing of featured elementary and secondary films with their corresponding curriculum area ties. The program presents another opportunity to thank sponsors.

- Signs to be used at the event provide to information regarding the films on demand—those available for viewing at the kiosks. They also supply information on locations of musical performances and direct the flow of people in the auditorium.

- Posters advertising the festival to be designed by digital art students.

Our posters are created by our high school students. We take one from each of our five high schools. Thanks to our sponsors, we are able to arrange for professional printing of the posters, invitations, VIP badges, and event programs at reduced rates.

Analyzing Films

In the weeks leading up to the event, a lot of film submission data must be analyzed. Once all of the films are submitted, there are many factors that come into consideration when selecting films for the big screen and sequencing them for the night of the festival. For our purposes, we have made the decision that any film that meets the requirements set in the *Entry Guide Booklet* will be included in the festival. Some of the factors we take into consideration when selecting top films for the big screen are the following:

- **Connection to the curriculum.** Does the film support learning goals from the district's curriculum?

- **Adherence to the guidelines.** Most important, does the film meet time limit and copyright guidelines? Do the filmmakers include citations of their resources?

- **Creative nature of the film.** Will it be entertaining to the audience?

- **Amount of follow-up work.** How much work will be involved in fixing problems with sound or images?

- **Representation of schools.** Are all schools represented?

- **Representation of curriculum areas.** Are all curriculum areas represented?

- **Representation of genres.** Do we have variety of types of films?

Deciding which films will be shown on the big screen is a time-intensive process. Over the years, we have tweaked our submission database to enable us to gather the data (factors to consider in the previous bulleted list) more efficiently. Nonetheless, our team (of 10) must watch all of the films, ask questions, and have in-depth conversations about each of the films. As a team we decide which films will be highlighted in the festival. The length of time this takes depends on the number of submissions we received. When you plan a film festival, be sure to carve out enough time in the overall schedule to allow for this important process to be completed. The amount of time needed is variable. We typically set aside three days for 150 or so videos. Sometimes we need more time; sometimes we get done early. This is done three weeks before the festival.

The next task after making the final selection of films for the big screen is creating a sequence for viewing. We take into consideration the following ideas when sequencing the films for the big screen.

Presentation Design

- Begin with several energetic, upbeat films to set the mood for the evening.

- The first and last films should be two of the strongest submissions, beginning and ending the festival on high notes.

- Intersperse the more serious films throughout the show to create ups and downs.

- Spread out multiple entries from one school by dispersing them throughout the show. Consider representing each school at least once toward the beginning of the evening so students and parents don't have to wait too long to see one of their school's films. This is especially important if there are a large number of elementary schools participating.

Logistics

Following is a logistics checklist. More detailed event planner checklists appear in Chapter 7 and contain suggestions for how many months ahead of the date of the festival tasks should be started.

Logistics Checklist

☐ Determine the best date and time for the festival in relation to the district's calendar (communicate with district administrators, sponsors, and partners). Sponsors are local business owners who contribute funds, materials, or services to the festival. Partners are teachers, staff members, students, and parents who volunteer to serve on committees and to do work on festival day.

☐ Select and establish the event location (if off campus consider the budget).

☐ Contact and confirm all contracts (venue, red carpet, partners).

☐ Plan and map out program schedule (walking the red carpet, vestibule entertainment for featured films).

☐ Coordinate film festival "brand" including logos, production and distribution of printed items (posters, invitations, programs, VIP badges, awards, related mailings).

☐ Arrange to have essential supplies available for distribution (entry guidelines, posters, digital communication, event programs).

☐ Identify each presenter's needs (emcee, technical booth operators, red carpet announcer, event host/hostess, ushers). Include technical infrastructure, placement, and arrange for volunteers and on-demand support via walkie-talkie.

☐ Verify venue layout requirements, such as band placement, red carpet, crowd management, kiosk set-up and tear-down, and raffle distribution. The core team's liaison will handle all items related to the festival venue.

☐ Anticipate additional needs—arrange for adequate host support throughout the event (extra film festival support: district/building technology facilitation committee members).

☐ Create the press kit, including the *Entry Guide Booklet* and materials from the precious year: event photographs, a DVD of top featured films, a VIP badge, and venue information and maps.

☐ Communicate, communicate, communicate (with students, teachers, administrators, district/building committees, partners, presenters, and team members).

Marketing and PR

As a team, it is important to establish marketing and public relations plans that ensure all involved parties are thinking about the film festival and planning for it in advance. The first and most important step in marketing the film festival is having conversations with curriculum coordinators, administrators, teachers, and students that result in their support and guaranteed participation. Without internal buy-in, there will be no festival. Once these integral members are on board, it will be time to sell the idea to external partners. We've found that a press kit showcasing

> ### Raffle
>
> Rather than provide gifts or handouts to every festival attendee, we solicit our sponsors for raffle prizes. A drawing is held during intermission. In the past we've had laptops, an Xbox, notebooks, video cameras, and so on.

the previous year's event to be a beneficial visual in our conversations with sponsors and partners. The press kit includes the *Entry Guide Booklet* and materials from the previous year's festival: event photographs, a DVD of top featured films, a VIP badge, and venue information and maps.

The members of the marketing and public relations group (made up, in our case, of the members of the Instructional Technology department with technology integration specialists in each building) focus their attention on attitudes toward the festival. They identify the guidelines and procedures that will meet the needs of all participants and guests and undertake the actions necessary to get an entire district to accept, understand, and participate in the festival. While our leadership team works on internal communication, publicity literature, partner relations, and community involvement, we also take on various behind-the-scenes activities. Our team monitors outcomes and fine tunes the festival with these overarching goals in mind: to celebrate all student participants and their creations, to improve curriculum integration techniques with teachers and students, and to work toward the next level of professional development.

In timing elements of the promotional campaign for the event, it is important to remember what to focus on at what times. In the months leading up to the submission deadline, promotional materials should focus on creating entries to the film festival. After the submission deadline, the focus of advertising shifts to attending the film festival.

> ### Student Volunteers?
>
> The festival is for students. We try not to give them a bunch of jobs. Rather, we want to celebrate them and let them enjoy it. There are a few exceptions such as a band playing in the atrium or some students taking paparazzi photos.

Once a support structure has been created for the film festival, there are several promotional tasks that will be necessary to build and maintain interest each year. Below are some of the strategies we implement to market participation in our film festival. A suggested time frame for these tasks and strategies is given in Chapter 7.

- Create/Update the *Entry Guide Booklet* to be used by teachers; it outlines submission guidelines and event details. In our case, we distribute one to each school library. (The *Entry Guide Booklet* details how to become involved in and prepare for particular special events for the festival, such as the

On-Demand Film kiosks, featured films, intermission entertainment, poster, presentation, raffle, and so forth.)

- Communicate with high school teachers who teach digital design in their art or graphic design courses to initiate student-created posters that will be used to advertise the film festival in the months leading up to the event.

- Create a short video announcing the film festival to be distributed via email.

- Promote the film festival through follow-up emails.

- Communicate with the public relations department to advertise in district and local community publications. If your district does not have a PR department, consult with the superintendent to locate a district administrator who can help with this task.

- Advertise during related professional development opportunities.

- Advertise at the building level through display cases, video announcements, newsletters, and so on.

Technical and Web Support

Producing a film festival requires that certain levels of technical and web support systems are in place. Locate people who can either support festival needs in-house or know where to locate the resources necessary to accomplish the technical side of the festival. In thinking about the technical aspects of the festival, be sure that someone is responsible for each of the following needs:

- Normalizing video and sound

- Rendering movies at a consistent size for best quality on a large screen

- Creating and utilizing databases that will be used for submissions

- Writing programs that support the needs of the festival

- Designing a website that promotes the festival and hosts resources

- Establishing QR (quick response) codes and mobile applications. (Each film festival poster contains a QR code; when the code is captured with the camera on a mobile device, it will take the user to the festival's mobile site.)

Normalizing and Rendering Video

Video submissions to the festival come in all sizes and qualities. One of the most laborious processes to be accomplished in postproduction is normalization. When teachers upload their videos and check them for the film festival, the videos are sent to the server as noncompressed files to maintain the highest levels of quality. Still, our students are using everything from camera phones to HD video cameras. Some are shot widescreen, while other videos are shot in standard 4:3 ratio. In order for all these films to look and sound good when they are played back to back at the festival, we need to normalize the audio and set the aspect ratio for each final, full-length film.

The first step in this is to pull all the videos off the server in their uncompressed states. The videos are sorted by categories for their final screenings at the festival: elementary, secondary, and the On-Demand Film kiosks. The videos are then all loaded into Adobe Premier. The project size is set to 720 × 480, as this is widescreen in standard definition. By setting this, all the films will be played within this window. Some will have black bars on their sides due to being shot and/or edited in a 4:3 ratio, but the playing surface itself on the screen will not change. This setting helps the videos flow from one to the next more fluidly. We also take the time to try to fix minor video editing issues that may be present, from lighting concerns to credit speed.

Once the entire video is pulled together, it is rendered and sent to Adobe Soundbooth. (The final export process is called rendering. This will create a file that can be viewed with a multimedia player on a variety of different computers.) With this tool, we can normalize the audio or make it sound even. Normalizing the video first for each clip is as simple as a click. This brings down the high levels and brings up the lows to be a little more even. It is also usually necessary to manually adjust certain sections of audio, bring them up or down to match the rest of the voices or sounds. Once an individual clip sounds good, we move on to the next and repeat. Once all the clips are normalized, we still need to bring the levels of all the clips into alignment. This involves bringing whole clips up or down to a nice mid-level. This saves us the trouble in the theater of needing to bring the volume up or down, depending upon the video clip being shown. We also try to remove extraneous noises, such as clicks, wind, and other background noises that take away from the clip.

Once all the clips have been leveled and edited, they are rendered from here and are ready to show. Each time we render a video, it is done in uncompressed DV-AVI format so as not to lose any quality. This makes for rather large files, upward of 60–80 gigabytes, for each half of the film festival (approximately one hour of video). The rendering also can take a great deal of time, depending on the power of the computer. As a rough guideline, count on from two to four times the actual playing time for rendering. That is, a two-minute video will take from four to eight minutes to render for sound quality.

Databases

A large portion of pulling off a successful film festival boils down to organization. The organization is a full-time job but can be automated through the use of databases; technology can make life easier but is not a requirement for creating this kind of a festival. Databases are used for the storage of film classification data (curriculum, grade level, privacy, etc.); metadata (unique identifier, video size/length, etc.); and associated student data (class, teacher, permissions, etc.). This data can be cross referenced for numerous purposes, including but not limited to populating credits lists, creating VIP badges, sequencing, and rendering. Minimally, a spreadsheet that lists student and teacher names, and video title will suffice.

Web Applications

A delivery system of sorts should be created not only to bring in finished films, but also to send out pertinent information to school district staff and the general public. To bring in videos, our district uses a system called Parkway Digital (see Chapter 3). This is a web application created in-house to manage submitted films and their corresponding students. Often such a system is beyond the reach of a school district, but there are other options for submitting films digitally, including establishing a YouTube channel or installing PHP Motion on a local server.

Promoting the Festival

To disseminate information, both printed and digital media are used. To continue the theme of having the festival be completely driven by student-created work, we ask the digital arts teachers in each building to have students create posters to advertise the festival across the district.

Figures 6.2, 6.3, and 6.4 Past posters advertising our film festival

Each of our five high schools creates posters with the pertinent information on them, and we post them all over the district and community (see Figures 6.2–6.4). On the night of the festival, we present each artist with a framed, poster-sized copy of his or her work as a way to say "thank you" for helping us to market the festival. This immediately gets all of the high schools involved and has proved to be very popular among students.

Additionally, a website is maintained and constantly updated with timely information (www.pkwy.k12.mo.us/tis/filmfestival). For example, upon initial announcement, the website contains links to our *Entry Guide Booklet*. After films are due, the website will change to house directions to the event and viewing location of films (big screen or On-Demand Film kiosk/s) as well as a link to the virtual gallery. During year three, we expanded our site and created a mobile version. Each film festival poster contains a QR code, or quick response code; when the code is captured with the camera on a mobile device, it will take the user to the mobile site. With the explosion in smartphones, it makes sense to harness the usage of mobile maps and video to disseminate information. There are numerous options for creating QR codes. For our festival, we use Google's Chart API through the use of Goo.gl (www.goo.gl), Google's URL shortener. By putting a ".qr" at the end of the shortened URL, a QR code is generated and can be used for promotional materials.

There are numerous checks built into the Parkway Digital system to guarantee against submission errors. Teachers are given information in real time as to any errors that may have occurred. This also alerts the Parkway Digital administrator and the building TIS so that any difficulties with receiving the films are greatly reduced. The goals are to speed assistance to submitting teachers as quickly as possible and to eliminate as many frustrations as possible. Making the technology get out of the way for the average teacher is our goal.

CHAPTER 7

Event Planners: Two Handy Checklists

Event planning is a skill unto itself. Planning a film festival—an event that culminates after months or even a year of work—might seem like an overwhelming prospect. We wrote this chapter to break down the planning process into completely manageable chunks. We've done the hard work so you don't have to!

At-a-Glance Planner

Months Out from Film Festival

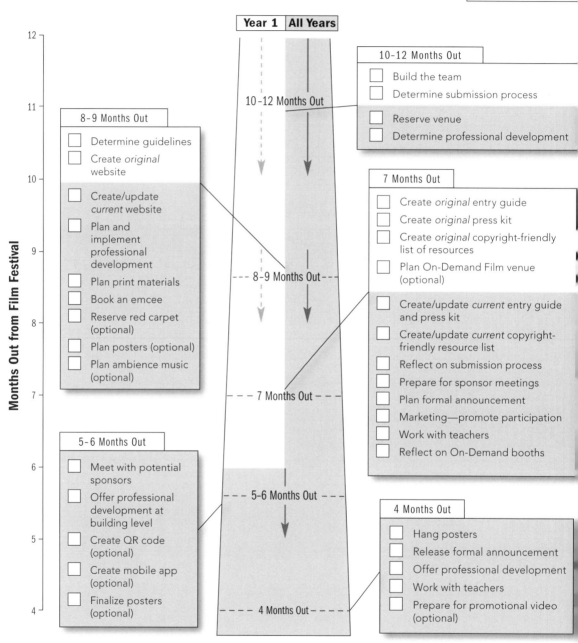

| Year 1 | All Years |

10–12 Months Out

- [ ] Build the team
- [ ] Determine submission process
- [ ] Reserve venue
- [ ] Determine professional development

8–9 Months Out

- [ ] Determine guidelines
- [ ] Create *original* website
- [ ] Create/update *current* website
- [ ] Plan and implement professional development
- [ ] Plan print materials
- [ ] Book an emcee
- [ ] Reserve red carpet (optional)
- [ ] Plan posters (optional)
- [ ] Plan ambience music (optional)

7 Months Out

- [ ] Create *original* entry guide
- [ ] Create *original* press kit
- [ ] Create *original* copyright-friendly list of resources
- [ ] Plan On-Demand Film venue (optional)
- [ ] Create/update *current* entry guide and press kit
- [ ] Create/update *current* copyright-friendly resource list
- [ ] Reflect on submission process
- [ ] Prepare for sponsor meetings
- [ ] Plan formal announcement
- [ ] Marketing—promote participation
- [ ] Work with teachers
- [ ] Reflect on On-Demand booths

5–6 Months Out

- [ ] Meet with potential sponsors
- [ ] Offer professional development at building level
- [ ] Create QR code (optional)
- [ ] Create mobile app (optional)
- [ ] Finalize posters (optional)

4 Months Out

- [ ] Hang posters
- [ ] Release formal announcement
- [ ] Offer professional development
- [ ] Work with teachers
- [ ] Prepare for promotional video (optional)

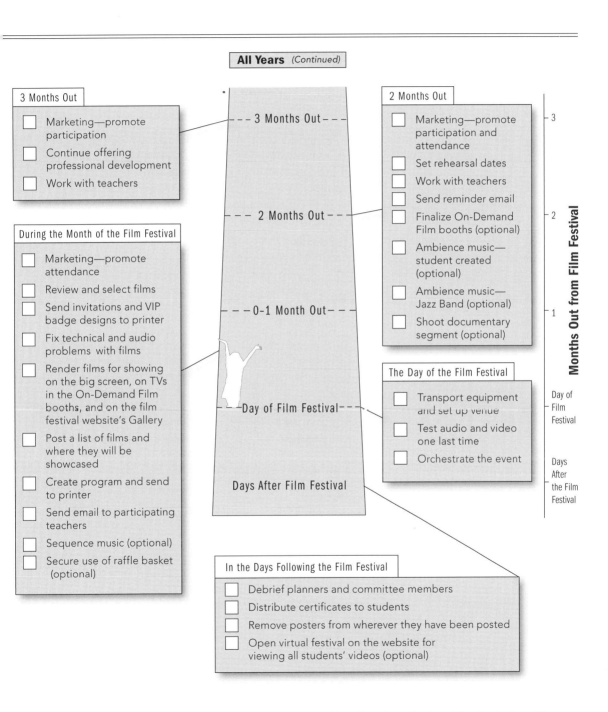

All Years *(Continued)*

3 Months Out
- ☐ Marketing—promote participation
- ☐ Continue offering professional development
- ☐ Work with teachers

During the Month of the Film Festival
- ☐ Marketing—promote attendance
- ☐ Review and select films
- ☐ Send invitations and VIP badge designs to printer
- ☐ Fix technical and audio problems with films
- ☐ Render films for showing on the big screen, on TVs in the On-Demand Film booths, and on the film festival website's Gallery
- ☐ Post a list of films and where they will be showcased
- ☐ Create program and send to printer
- ☐ Send email to participating teachers
- ☐ Sequence music (optional)
- ☐ Secure use of raffle basket (optional)

- - - 3 Months Out - - -

- - - 2 Months Out - - -

- - - 0-1 Month Out - - -

- - Day of Film Festival - - -

Days After Film Festival

2 Months Out
- ☐ Marketing—promote participation and attendance
- ☐ Set rehearsal dates
- ☐ Work with teachers
- ☐ Send reminder email
- ☐ Finalize On-Demand Film booths (optional)
- ☐ Ambience music— student created (optional)
- ☐ Ambience music— Jazz Band (optional)
- ☐ Shoot documentary segment (optional)

The Day of the Film Festival
- ☐ Transport equipment and set up venue
- ☐ Test audio and video one last time
- ☐ Orchestrate the event

In the Days Following the Film Festival
- ☐ Debrief planners and committee members
- ☐ Distribute certificates to students
- ☐ Remove posters from wherever they have been posted
- ☐ Open virtual festival on the website for viewing all students' videos (optional)

Months Out from Film Festival
— 3
— 2
— 1
Day of Film Festival
Days After the Film Festival

Two Event Planners, One Timeline

In preparing a checklist of items to be accomplished as the film festival is planned, we realized that having the film festival in the spring, like we do, may not be what is best for all schools or districts. As a result, we have tried to break it down by how many months away from the date of the festival each item should be addressed. Think of it as a countdown to the big day—whatever date on the calendar that may be.

Within each time section, there are tasks that will only have to be addressed during that first year ("Year 1" in the planner). There are also annual tasks to accomplish during the initial year and each year thereafter ("All Years" in the planner). The tasks marked "optional" are details that we have found enhance the event, but they are not crucial. While many of these ideas and tasks may be addressed in more detail in other areas of the book, the descriptions here are given simply to clarify and tie these ideas together.

At-a-Glance Planner

The At-a-Glance Planner at the beginning of this chapter is a handy reproducible reference meant to be used in conjunction with the Event Planner that follows.

Event Planner

For an overview of task timelines, see the At-a-Glance Planner (pages 86–87). For explanations, descriptions, and details of these tasks, see the Event Planner (pages 89–101). Tasks for the first year (Year 1) are not shaded. Year-1 tasks occur 7 to 12 months out. Tasks for All Years begin 12 months out and end in the days following the festival.

Event Planner

Year 1	10-12 Months Out
	✕ 10 11 12

☐ **Build the team**

The first step during the initial year is to build a team and decide which members will take on which tasks. In our case, we began this process a year before our first festival. This was the most difficult year because we tried to figure out how we wanted this festival to look as we went along. Many tasks were taken care of at the last minute. However, each year the planning and work leading up to the festival have gone more smoothly and have become more streamlined. It is crucial during the initial year to have conversations with the administrators in the school/district to ensure that they are on board from curricular and financial standpoints. This support system is necessary as the idea of the film festival trickles down to the teachers.

☐ **Determine submission process**

As a team, decide what method teachers will use to submit films for review. Our system was built in-house by one of the members of the instructional technology team and has served us well.

All Years	10-12 Months Out
	✕ 10 11 12

☐ **Reserve venue**

Select the date for the festival and reserve the venue as soon as possible. It is important to take into consideration the other events happening during that same time period. Depending on the time of year, be sure to avoid scheduling conflicts with parent/teacher conferences, finals, and standardized testing. We also avoid the evening before a long weekend, knowing that many families may begin traveling then. While it is never easy to find a downtime in educational calendars, offering the festival when the most parties can attend will help it to be as successful as possible.

☐ **Determine professional development**

Begin thinking about what professional development opportunities are needed for teachers who may participate. Determining what a well-rounded tech integration curriculum looks like in relation to district needs and the film festival is certainly a first step. Reflecting on the difficulties teachers have faced in having their students create digital stories, develop courses that will help to close these gaps for teachers. We have found that offering courses that address Web 2.0 tools, video production, digital storytelling, Marzano strategies, digital citizenship, and social media have helped teachers to understand the video creation process and the learning outcomes that are achieved through digital storytelling.

Year 1	8-9 Months Out
	☒ ☐ ☐ ☐ ☐ ☐ ☐ 8 9 ☐ ☐

☐ **Determine guidelines**

During the initial year, it will be important to determine the guidelines that students will use while creating projects to be shared at the festival. Knowing what criteria are being looked for and what will make the festival a successful display of student work are necessary before approaching teachers with the idea.

Guidelines to consider may include copyright compliance, tie to curriculum, and maximum length of films. Be sure to supply printed copies of these guidelines to each teacher or school in addition to having them posted online. We supply these guidelines printed in the form of an *Entry Guide Booklet*. The entry guide contains the mission of the film festival and how it aligns with the district's mission, the guidelines that should be followed by teachers and students, information about filmmaking, a list of our sponsors, and the event information. After the initial festival, a necessary extra step is to create a press kit, including your entry guide and a DVD of the previous year's film festival—useful tools for informing potential sponsors. (Creating a press kit is listed as a separate step under "7 Months Out.")

☐ **Create original website**

Creating a website for the festival and keeping it updated ensures that all parties involved have a resource to access at any time. The website should not only have all the festival information for marketing purposes, but also house any helpful resources that teachers and students can utilize as they work through the creation and submission process. It should act as a one-stop shop for all information relating to the film festival. Our 2012 site can be found at www.pkwy.k12.mo.us/tis/filmfestival/vGallery/?y=2012.

All Years	8-9 Months Out
	☒ ☐ ☐ ☐ ☐ ☐ ☐ 8 9 ☐ ☐

☐ **Update/create current website**

☐ **Plan and implement professional development**

Once the professional development needs have been determined, the planning of these courses can begin. Ensuring that these courses are offered with enough time for teachers to implement the filmmaking process in their classrooms is crucial. Teachers will need to feel comfortable planning and beginning projects with their students as creating videos fits into their curricular units. In the Parkway district, our Instructional Technology Department personnel teach these courses and schedule them based on the needs of the teachers in specific buildings. Typically, we offer approximately 12 to 20 hours district-wide each semester in addition to the support from the technology integration specialists in each building. Smaller districts may need to use their technology professionals to teach large groups of teachers at in-service sessions based on the technical ability and resources that the district has available.

Plan print materials

At this time, begin thinking about the printed materials needed to market the festival. In our case, this includes the following items: *Entry Guide Booklets*, posters, invitations, VIP badges, programs, and stickers. Consider whether the school or district has these printing capabilities or whether professional printing services are a better option. Also, be sure to consider the volume of printing, the quality, and color versus black and white. Professional printing can be costly and will probably require funding from sponsors. During our first two years, we had separate invitations and VIP badges. The invitations went to everyone involved, whereas only the students with films on the big screen received VIP badges. In an effort to be more inclusive in our celebration of all students who submitted their work, we decided that all students who participated in the film festival, with videos on the big screen or in the kiosks, should have VIP badges. As this was going to increase our printing costs dramatically, we decided to combine the invitation with the VIP badge. We did have a small number of separate invitation postcards printed to mail to non-district parties (see page 98, "During the Month of the Film Festival: Send invitations and VIP badge designs to printer" for more details).

Book an emcee

Who will emcee the event? Contact that person well in advance to make sure he or she is available and willing. This person may or may not be a member of the team. From the first year, we have used an emcee from the HEC-TV station that we partner with to air our festival. This became a natural fit for us because she is the producer/reporter who produces our student documentaries. It works well for us not to use a member of our team so that we are available to handle the other demands of the evening. We also liked the idea that this would once again not make us a focus of the evening, keeping as much focus on the students as possible.

Reserve red carpet (optional)

To give the event a rock star appeal, a good start is a red carpet. Visit the venue, plan for its placement, and measure for the appropriate length. Reserve it with a local party supply store as soon as possible to ensure availability.

Plan posters (optional)

In an effort to make our festival as student centered as possible, we have students create the posters that will advertise the festival. We approach the graphic design teacher from each high school to discuss the poster project and have them begin the assignment with their students. The posters will be due in about two months. It is imperative to get this project started early to give the students time to create, to allow the team time to finalize the design by adding the sponsors, and to allow time for printing and distribution. We hang posters in all of our schools and district buildings.

☐ **Plan ambience music (optional)**

At this time, a music technology teacher in the district is approached to discuss the use of original student musical compositions to be used the night of the film festival. Our student-created music is played in the theater during the intermission and in the lobby throughout the evening. The music teacher tells students that their work will be used at the film festival and collects student projects throughout the year.

Year 1	**7 Months Out**
	☐ ☐ ☐ ☐ ☐ 7 ☐ ☐ ☐ ☐

☐ **Create original entry guide**

One of the first tasks at this point is to create the entry guide that teachers will use as a resource when having their students engage in video projects that will be submitted. The entry guide includes the festival's mission as it aligns with the school's or district's mission, guidelines for entering, and ideas to help in project planning. We also include the date, time, and location of the festival along with a map to the venue.

☐ **Create original press kit**

The press kit will be an integral piece in securing sponsorship of your festival. The press kit should include the artifacts that will give potential sponsors a sense of the educational and emotional impact the festival has on students. Our press kit includes a copy of the *Entry Guide Booklet*, a postcard invitation, a student VIP badge, and a DVD of the previous year's films.

☐ **Create an original list of copyright-friendly resources**

Providing a list of web links to resources that are safe to use for the film festival relieves some of the burden from the teachers. It is important to house this document not only on the film festival website, but also in a location where teachers can easily find it for any multimedia projects they may be working on with students. Because this document alleviates the need for teachers to investigate the terms of use on their own, we make a point of having discussions with teachers that help to reinforce the difference between "fair use" and "copyright compliant." While some festivals operate under the Fair Use Guidelines, we require that all films be copyright compliant, due to our partnership with HEC-TV and the fact that we extend our festival by making all of the films available online.

☐ **Plan On-Demand Film venue (optional)**

Another logistical consideration is how to showcase work that doesn't make it to the big screen. We have chosen to use an On-Demand Film booth (also called a kiosk) where students, parents, and teachers can see students' work on smaller screens set up in the lobby. We use 40" flat-screen TVs that we borrow from schools within our district. Planning and arranging for this equipment and its set-up should begin now.

All Years	7 Months Out
	☒ [ ][ ][ ][ ] 7 [ ][ ][ ][ ]

☐ **Create/update current entry guide and current press kit**

To assure that the entry guide is current, replace older photos with pictures from the previous year's film festival, and revisit and revise text when needed to ensure that the mission of the film festival aligns with the district's mission. This also applies to the artifacts in the press kit.

☐ **Create/update current copyright-friendly resource list**

Although this is a working document that we add to throughout the year as we find new resources, it is at this time in the year that we make a point to make sure it is updated and all of the links are active.

☐ **Reflect on submission process**

In addition to the entry guide and press kit, we also reflect on and revise the submission process. Each year we tweak the process a bit to make things easier on us and the teachers. Using feedback from those submitting films, we look for ways to make the process more seamless and time efficient. We also consider what information we need to gather that will enable us to be efficient in using the database to sort information once all of the films have been submitted.

☐ **Prepare for sponsor meetings**

Identifying which businesses and community members might be interested in sponsoring the festival needs to be done early. In preparation for meeting with potential sponsors, in addition to the press kit, it will also be important to prepare a wish list of what will be needed to make it a success. Items to consider include the venue rental fee, red carpet rental, printing costs, poster frames, raffle prizes, and certificate foil seals and paper. It is important to secure adequate sponsorship at this point in the year to ensure accurate planning for the film festival. At the same time, it's also a good idea to start approaching sponsors about donating items that can be used in a raffle for participating students on the night of the festival. (All students who participate in the festival get entered into the raffle drawing.)

☐ **Plan formal announcement**

Planning for the formal announcement of the film festival to the district needs to be started. We use a promotional video that is sent out to all of the schools in our district. Production of this video starts with the brainstorming of design ideas and assigning roles to the team. Once complete, an email containing the video announcement is sent out to the district from a team email address, and the film festival season officially begins.

☐ **Marketing—promote participation**

Marketing for the festival continues with presentations at school faculty meetings, building and district-level technology committee meetings, and classrooms. These presentations include showing the film festival website and what it has to offer, our district database where district-created films are housed for sharing, and some examples of films created in previous years that are well done and show a clear tie to the curriculum. Sharing video clips from last year's festival that highlight the venue and show students on the red carpet helps to build excitement among teachers and students.

☐ **Work with teachers**

The official kickoff signals that it is time for the Technology Team to work with teachers on planning and implementing digital projects in their classrooms. This starts with identifying units in the curriculum that lend themselves to video creation and brainstorming implementation ideas. This work continues until the submission due date.

☐ **Reflect on On-Demand Film booths/kiosks**

Each year we think about the success of the On-Demand Film booth. During our first two years, we used two booths to loop the elementary films that were not playing on the big screen. Each kiosk looped half of the elementary films. We used a third booth to loop all of the secondary films that were not being shown on the big screen. A sign indicated which films were playing on which TV and in what order. It became apparent that this format was not working well for our audience. Students and their families who came to see their films at the kiosk had to wait 40 minutes for the video file to loop around. Although our mission was to celebrate all students and not have our festival be a competition, this quickly made students feel like they were second place. We knew the kiosks needed to change. We decided to have four areas for viewing that were interactive so that students could pick their film to watch in addition to any others they might be interested in seeing. We accomplished this by using interactive monitors that we borrowed from a sponsor as the interface for students to choose their film and view it on a 40" flat-screen TV. This change transformed our festival into an event rather than just a screening.

All Years	5-6 Months Out
	✕ 5 6

☐ **Meet with potential sponsors**

About six months from the festival, it is time to schedule and meet with representatives of potential sponsors. These meetings include not only discussing the purpose of the film festival and what the event entails, but also possible joint effort marketing initiatives. What can we do for each other? In response to their sponsorship, we offer to advertise for them on our website, on the posters and VIP badges, in the entry guide, and in the event programs. Depending on what the sponsor is able to donate, conversations are adapted. We have different sponsors that donate funding, materials (such as lanyards), and items to be raffled. However, it is our partnership with the Higher

Education Channel (HEC-TV), a local cable TV station, that has really elevated our film festival to the next level by providing an even greater audience for our students' work. A lot of preplanning takes place in our November meeting with HEC-TV. Ideas are discussed for the "Behind the Minds" segment that precedes the film festival. This segment showcases the students at work on their entries to highlight the learning that takes place during the creation process.

☐ **Offer professional development at building level**

At this point in the year, in addition to our district-level courses, our team begins to offer some additional development sessions to teachers in their individual buildings. These are planned based on building needs and may include showcasing a new digital storytelling tool each month. Work with teachers on an individual basis (during their free periods and before and after school) continues also.

☐ **Create QR code (optional)**

Using a free, online QR code creator, we make a QR code that we have printed on the posters and the invitations; the code directs mobile device users to the mobile app website for our festival.

☐ **Create mobile app (optional)**

Our mobile app website includes a link to general information about the film festival, our introduction video, and directions to the venue. Because QR codes are fairly new, we have also included information about QR codes and their capabilities on the film festival website.

☐ **Finalize posters (optional)**

Final approval of posters should also be done at the six-month mark. The team adds the sponsor banner (or sponsors' banners) to the bottom of the design and includes a QR code that directs users to a film festival mobile site. The posters need to be sent to the printer so that they can be displayed in schools for marketing purposes. At this time, the new poster graphics are also added to the entry guide master file so that updated *Entry Guide Booklets* can be printed and distributed to schools.

All Years	4 Months Out
	✕ 4

☐ **Hang posters**

We make sure to hang at least one poster of each design in each building in our district. Larger buildings may get two of each design. These should remain hanging until after the film festival.

☐ **Release formal announcement**

Send an "all staff" email announcing the official opening to the film festival season. This email includes the introduction video, which not only reminds staff of the film festival details but also announces the opening of the submission window.

☐ **Offer professional development**

Continue offering building/district-level development opportunities.

☐ **Work with teachers**

Continue working with individual teachers on digital storytelling projects.

☐ **Prepare for promotional video ("Behind the Minds") (optional)**

Through our partnership with HEC-TV, a documentary featuring our students is created that highlights the process students engage in to create their films. Begin to think about students and projects that will help convey and promote the spirit of the festival. Students will be actively creating videos when shooting begins. Begin to contact teachers to set up dates for filming. A partnership with a TV station isn't crucial to accomplishing this, as we have produced a similar piece on our own in past years to showcase the learning that goes into the final products.

All Years	3 Months Out
	✕ ⬚3⬚ ⬚⬚⬚⬚⬚⬚⬚⬚⬚⬚

☐ **Marketing—promote participation**

Continue marketing through all schools and district media that is available. Consider face-to-face reminders at committee and staff meetings as well as "all staff" email reminders. The email that we send at this point also links to a video that gives tips on how to get started with a project. Also utilize electronic and paper newsletters at both the district and school levels. Other ideas to consider may be decorating bulletin boards or display cases and advertising through school slide shows and PA announcements.

☐ **Continue offering professional development**

Continue offering building/district-level development opportunities.

☐ **Work with teachers**

Continue working with individual teachers on digital storytelling projects.

All Years	2 Months Out
	✕ ⬚2⬚ ⬚⬚⬚⬚⬚⬚⬚⬚⬚

☐ **Marketing—promote participation and attendance**

Continue marketing the festival in the school/district and in the community as well. Within the school or district, the goal is to continue encouraging participation. In the community, the marketing strategy is about promoting attendance. Give people time to get it on their calendars and make plans to attend. Some outlets to consider are the school or district website and any school or district publications, such as newsletters, and local newspapers and other media sources. We work closely with the district's public relations department to promote the festival throughout the year.

☐ **Set rehearsal dates**

Be sure to contact the venue representative to schedule rehearsal dates. The rehearsal times are used to plan use of the space, including the lobby/foyer and the theater seating area for the evening. This is also a time for tech team members to meet with the technical representatives of the venue. The techs will run the audiovisual booth for the evening and will need to coordinate with the venue's team on the use of equipment and the order of the evening. Additionally, use this rehearsal time to do a last-minute check of the audio and video quality on the equipment. If the rehearsal is scheduled a few days in advance, there will still be time to correct audio levels before the big night.

☐ **Work with teachers**

Work with teachers becomes more about finalizing and publishing projects than beginning them. Many teachers will begin to look for assistance in submitting films. Remind everyone that students' video submissions are due in one month.

☐ **Send reminder email**

Send an "all staff" email to keep the film festival in the forefront of teachers' minds.

☐ **Finalize On-Demand Film booths (optional)**

Solidify plans for the films that are not shown on the big screen. Knowing how to manage this footage before the submission deadline is imperative. Once the review process for films begins, there will not be much turnaround time to get all of the technical logistics accomplished. During our first two festivals, we had these booths on a continuous video loop. Switching to the on-demand system and giving attendees viewing choices created a lot more work but was well worth it.

☐ **Ambience music—student created (optional)**

At this time we touch base with the music technology teacher/s again to ensure that they know when we will need the music (about a week before the festival) in order to prepare the CD that will be played in the lobby and during the intermission.

☐ **Ambience music—jazz band (optional)**

Consider whether a school or district jazz band will play as families arrive and students walk the red carpet. This adds yet another way to showcase students and enhances the atmosphere of the evening. Securing the band will need to be done at this time. Also take into consideration how this will impact the kiosk area in terms of sound and acoustics.

☐ **Shoot documentary segment (optional)**

Visit classrooms to film students working on digital storytelling projects to capture the process and collaborative conversations that go into the creation of a film. Conduct interviews with the teachers and students to gain further insights on the educational value of this type of project. Videos of students working on projects are great tools for getting buy-in from teachers and administrators.

All Years	During the Month of the Film Festival
	☒ 1 ☐ ☐ ☐ ☐ ☐ ☐ ☐ ☐ ☐ ☐

☐ **Marketing—promote attendance**

Now that the submission deadline has passed, the marketing strategy becomes solely about promoting attendance. Make information about the film festival accessible in as many places as possible so that community members, staff, parents, and students all are aware of the event. Ideas to consider include an announcement on the schools' and district's websites, an announcement at a Board of Education meeting, continued posting of pertinent information in newsletters, and alerting local media. Record and distribute audio PSAs for local media use.

☐ **Review and select films**

Submissions should be due about a month before the festival to give the team time to prepare the films. Begin reviewing the films as soon as possible after the due date. The amount of time needed to block out for the team to work together to select the films depends on how many films are submitted. With 150–200 submissions, we can review films over a three-day period. During this time, we watch every film, taking into consideration many factors. We look for a tie to the curriculum, entertainment value, creativity, adherence to the time limit, and copyright compliance. Many times the TISs from particular buildings can give some background about their students' films. Based on all this information, we decide whether each submission should go to the big screen, to the On-Demand Film booth, or if we should revisit it later when we have watched all of the other films. In the end, time is a determining factor. We only have so much time at the theater, so it is not physically possible to show every film. In our case, we break up the festival into two one-hour sections—one for elementary and one for secondary. By limiting show time to two hours, we can highlight films from a variety of schools and classes while still maintaining audience interest.

☐ **Send invitations and VIP badge designs to printer**

Whether these are two separate documents or combined as one, as discussed under "8–9 Months Out: Plan print materials," it is important to get these to the printer as soon as possible so that they can be distributed to schools and sent home to parents. We give a VIP badge to every student whose film is being shown at the festival no matter which venue. To honor students in this way, the number will vary depending on the number of students who participate. This cannot be determined until after all submitted films have been reviewed. We also give VIP badges to students who created posters and music, all building and district administrators, all curriculum coordinators, and members of the Board of Education. Invitations are mailed to the PTO presidents for all buildings, teachers who have sponsored films, and local government officials.

☐ **Fix technical and audio problems with films**

Part of preparing the films for the big screen is to take films that were created using different kinds of equipment and cleaning up their audio and video for presentation. For us, this involves going through each video with a sound-editing program to reduce ambient noise and static pops while normalizing the volume levels from film to film. While this process is time consuming, the event itself is significantly improved because the films all have good sound quality. Additionally, we look for dropped video frames or blurry images. Anything we can fix before putting all of the films together is done in the weeks prior to the festival itself.

☐ **Render films (on big screen, TVs, On-Demand Film booths, etc.)**

We made the decision early on that we wanted the night of the festival to be a high-quality production. Adding simple things like title slides before each video and combining all videos into one file that can be played from beginning to end helps us do that. After each film is "fixed," we place it in the correct order for the showcase and render it as one high-quality video. This practice eliminates the need for switching files and creates a seamless show for the audience. Each of these finalized files (one for the elementary students' videos and one for the secondary students' videos) is approximately one hour long and can take as much as 60 GB of storage space. This type of file can take up to eleven hours to render, so in your planning, be sure to allot ample time to compile the final video.

☐ **Post a list of films and where they will be showcased**

As soon as a final list has been created for each of the venues (Virtual—on the film festival's Internet Gallery; On-Demand Films—on TV screens in the festival's kiosks; and Highlighted—on the festival's big screen), it is crucial to get this list published. Teachers and students will be anxious to have this information as soon as possible. We publish this information on our website and send the link to participating teachers in an email. To stress the idea that the festival is all inclusive, we publish a complete list for each venue. In this way, films are duplicated on a number of lists so the focus isn't on where that film is not playing; instead, we hope to say, "Look at all the places the film *is* playing."

☐ **Create program and send to printer**

Once the films that will be shown on the big screen have been selected, it is time to finalize the program and get it sent to the printer. Our program includes our film festival's mission statement, the URL to our department's website for more information and the URL for the virtual festival, "Save the Date" for next year's festival, information on when the films can be seen on TV through our partnership with HEC-TV, the order of films on the big screen organized by elementary and secondary, and a page to recognize festival sponsors and the district's board members and superintendents.

☐ **Send email to participating teachers**

Send an email to participating teachers as soon as the published list of films is completed. In this email we include a "thank you" to teachers for submitting their students' work, a link to the published list of films telling at which venue each will be showcased, a PDF attachment of a "Save the Date" flyer to be sent home with participating students, and a trailer video of films that will be featured on the big screen.

☐ **Sequence music (optional)**

The music that is submitted to us by the students in our district's Music Technology class is sequenced into an order that flows nicely as it plays in the lobby throughout the evening and during the intermission in the auditorium.

☐ **Secure use of raffle basket (optional)**

If a live raffle is planned, secure the use of a raffle basket for the evening. The basket holds the names of all participating students. Some schools may have a raffle basket to use for carnivals and other fund-raising events.

All Years	The Day of the Film Festival

☐ **Transport equipment and set up venue**

Be sure to plan plenty of time for setting up the venue. Rolling out the red carpet, setting up On-Demand Film booths, preparing the big screen films, and situating everything "just so" takes time. We give ourselves about 2 hours to be sure everything is set up before the first families begin to arrive.

☐ **Test audio and video one last time**

Testing the audio for the student-created music, the big-screen films, and the microphone for the emcee should all be done before the doors open.

☐ **Orchestrate the event**

During the festival itself, all team members should actively play a role in the production of the event.

All Years	In the Days Following the Film Festival
	☒ □ □ □ □ □ □ □ □ □ □ □

☐ **Debrief planners and committee members**

Reflection is always a good idea after an event such as this. Every year we take some time on the day after the festival to think about what worked and what didn't as well as to brainstorm ideas for the following year. Just as we ask students to reflect on their films, it behooves us to reflect on the event itself.

☐ **Distribute certificates to students**

In addition to VIP badges, all students who submit a film get a certificate of participation. Rather than trying to pass these out at the event itself, we choose to deliver them to teachers for distribution in the days following the event.

☐ **Remove posters from wherever they have been posted**

☐ **Open virtual festival on the website (optional)**

The final venue is the virtual festival that will be archived and showcased online on the festival's website. This piece of the festival is opened on the day after the event. Hoping to draw on some of the excitement from the previous night, we tell students and teachers that all films can be viewed online from that point forward. Additionally, we advertise the TV special that will showcase all of the big screen films on HEC-TV (www.hectv.org). To see a video about the 2012 Parkway Digital Film Festival produced by HEC-TV, visit www.hectv.org/programs/series/parkway-digital-film-fest/1677/part-4-2012.

CHAPTER 8

Making Movies

*The entire process of creating videos in the classroom
can be a daunting one for teachers and students alike.
It can be complicated to navigate copyrights and
media formats and to gain technical expertise; however,
it can also be extremely rewarding for students as
they take ownership of their own learning. Each
choice that students make in the movie making
process must be a conscious attempt to move their
stories along and make connections to the curriculum.
Without that connection, filmmaking is just another
activity done in isolation. Will bad movies be made?
Absolutely. But until bad movies are made, there are no
movies, and those students' stories may never be told.*

Audience, Purpose, and Story

The process of incorporating video into the classroom is one of discovery. Like any other creative endeavor, in order to get better at creating videos, one has to create videos—and lots of them. Techniques need to be refined and explored, and the process must be flexible enough to give students freedom that allows for experimentation. One way to approach this is to help students make connections with other processes they have learned and experienced. In this case, we liken the journey of video creation to that of the writing process; videos are created in three stages: preproduction, production, and postproduction. While this book is not meant to be a comprehensive how-to manual for teaching digital storytelling, this chapter outlines techniques we have used as we've worked with students at each stage of the production process.

Preproduction: *The Story Begins*

The journey through the creation process begins by employing storytelling techniques as students plan their movies. Preproduction is a time when students participate in brainstorming ideas, scriptwriting to determine the depth of their content understanding, peer editing for fluency, storyboarding to provide the blueprint for production, and practicing of responsible copyright usage. The first decision to be made can be done by students, the teacher, or both. The audience and purpose of the digital project must be defined. Who will be the primary audience for the message? Is it going to be instructional, informational, a documentary, a public service announcement, or a fictional story? These decisions serve as guiding points for the remainder of this process. As decisions are made throughout the subsequent stages, if they contradict the audience or purpose, they need to be revisited. Once the purpose has been determined, students can begin collecting and brainstorming ideas that support it.

The next step is to start scripting and to begin thinking about the storyboard. These two items can be done simultaneously because the script is about the message, and the description and the storyboard are about the visual story. When students focus on telling a story, they begin to think about their content area differently. Instead of a book report in which facts, figures, and explanations are the basis for their film, student must think about the decisions they make so they can communicate with their audience and the purpose of the video. Focusing clearly on audience and purpose will lead to successful storytelling through a digital lens.

Scripts/Drafts

Scripting is essential to storytelling, as it represents the concept learned. It also provides the place where students can determine their audience and think about the message they want to share. An important piece of this is to encourage students to use curricular vocabulary if appropriate (such as in a content area like math or science) and to think about the way they want to engage the audience. For example, in an eighth grade science class where students are studying hurricanes, the purpose could be informational with the focus on impact in the communities. While creating the story, students can sprinkle in vocabulary words from the unit, such as "eye of the storm," to help demonstrate understanding. The vocabulary shouldn't be a word-for-word definition memorized in class; it should harmonize with the story's context and create a perspective or point of view. Encouraging students to write scripts individually and to pitch their ideas to the teacher and the rest of their group allows for a variety of ideas to be brought to the table, giving each member input. This work should not be done in isolation but in collaboration, where students can discuss and refine ideas together. Some questions to get students thinking about digital stories might include the following:

- Using what other perspectives could you tell your story?

- How could you add emotion through audio, music, or lighting?

- What do you want your audience to be able to tell us about the project you created?

Some visual students may find it difficult to begin writing immediately; they may be more comfortable plotting out the pictures first on their storyboards and then beginning the scripting after they see their story materialize on paper. As students write, have them think about their favorite TV shows and what keeps them coming back to see more of those shows. Transferring that interest to their scripts helps them make connections to their own work and to analyze storytelling techniques that they might want to employ.

Once individual scripts are finished, peer-editing groups can determine whether the writer's intended message is evident and fluent. Giving someone else the script and asking the person to determine what the message is can be beneficial to fulfilling the goals of the final product and can be a checkpoint for formative assessment. After refinements to the scripts and storyboards are made, assemble groups according to similar scripts and encourage collaboration to determine which of the scripts best represents its story's message. After the script has been chosen by the group, the teacher can review it to be sure it meets the learning objectives.

Scripting and storyboarding are key elements in the planning process. Following are some topics that can be used as conversation starters in the drafting and script editing process:

- How does the video evoke emotion (music, photos, sound effects, etc.)?

- How does curricular vocabulary transfer into the production of the story?

- What elements will stay true to the message and audience while engaging emotions (action verbs, mannerisms, nonverbal cues, fluency, pronunciation and voice, body language)?

- Does the script reflect a fluent message?

- Is the movie appropriate for the targeted audience?

- How does the movie get the audience emotionally involved in the topic?

- What types of filming/technical elements will keep the movie varied and flowing (shots, angles, pace, etc.)?

- Is this work original, or does it too closely mimic something that has been done before?

- Is the video's main idea/message clear?

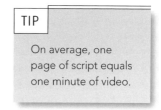

TIP

On average, one page of script equals one minute of video.

At each step in the process, students need teacher/peer approval to ensure that the work is a high-quality production and that learning objectives are met.

Peer Editing

As a part of the preproduction process, students need the opportunity to analyze their own and others' works to reflect upon and ultimately improve their own and peers' scripts. This will look different at different grade levels, but the idea remains the same. The peer-editing process allows for a look at different methods of telling the story by offering multiple perspectives.

When editing in content areas, check that the work has continuity and reflects that the material was learned or that the writer understood the learning objectives and communicated them through the plot, characters' dialogues, and narrative. Students can read each others' scripts to decide whether they convey clear messages and fluent stories. If students can summarize the main points of a peer's story accurately, the script probably has a clear message. However, just because the story is clear, it may not meet the objectives of the project.

Teachers should always give final approval to scripts, but as a part of peer editing, students should be aware of the learning objectives and give feedback based on those criteria as well. During this part of preproduction, it's a good idea for teachers to model what kind of elements to be looking for in the story. Too often, students will focus on one element (technical details, characters, or plot) rather than looking at the whole picture. By scaffolding those skills, students will give more meaningful feedback to their classmates whether on an individual level or as an entire class project.

Peer editing and writers' responses to suggestions by making revisions are the final steps of script writing before students can start collecting resources and moving into production. To decide if the script is ready to be put into production, consider whether or not the topic is supported with details and clearly shows a beginning, middle, and end. Does the topic lack connection because it is not fully developed, awkward, or lacks a connection to the objectives being learned? Much like writing, the revision process is continual and will not end here; however, this is the point at which a green light is given to begin planning the specifics of production.

Storyboards

Storyboards are a key component to quality video production; they provide information such as, shot angles, scene location, dialogue, music, background noise, sound effects, transition, and effects. This is the blueprint for sequencing the events' visual materials and interactions with the voiceovers and images that create the most coherent message. The storyboard allows students to take the script and break it up into scenes where they talk about place, characters, transitions, and logical presentation of the story. This is another important area where examples of storyboards can greatly help students. Teachers can find many examples online of storyboards from actual movies. A simple YouTube or Flickr search will bring hundreds of results of actual storyboards used in productions.

Storyboard Strategies

- Use one index card per scene

- Use an online storyboard: http://kidsvid.4teachers.org

- Create a blank, three-slide PowerPoint and select "print 3 slides" to sheet

- Create a grid in Word that contains columns for the clip number, scene, people and places description, and conditions and effects (lighting and sound)

- Give students a digital camera to frame pictures of actual locations (lack of artistic skill is not a barrier)

Gathering Copyright-Friendly Resources

A wide range of views pertaining to the use of copyright in education can be found; the spectrum goes from quite liberal to very conservative. Copyright plays an important role in our film festival, as the videos are shown in a public forum with a real audience and are made available on the Higher Education Channel (HEC), a local access television station, as well as online—on HEC's website and on Parkway's Digital Film Festival website via its Gallery. Our school district's conservative stance on the use of copyrighted materials is that all student materials must be originally created, labeled as Creative Commons/public domain with attribution, or be confirmed through proof of permission. Adherence to these guidelines removes the burden of any legal concerns for our festival and models digital citizenship. We make a conscious effort to educate teachers, other education specialists, and students on the appropriate use of images, sounds, and other media they may use. In this way, students are able to tell their stories with a multitude of sources while practicing responsible use and appropriate ownership.

When working with library media specialists, teachers, and students our goal is to teach ethical use and ownership rather than copyright law. The approach is simple: how can students ethically find digital resources to use in their stories? As a part of this campaign, we have some strategies that help teachers address these issues.

- Limiting the palette from which students may choose their resources

- Limiting usage to specific sites that fall under our usage guidelines

- Using the advanced search tool in Google

- Encouraging conversations about copyright and ownership with students
- Obtaining permissions before using certain resources
- Creating original pieces of work

Some teachers use a reference sheet that was created specifically for the film festival and allows students to use any of the resources on that list as long as attribution is given. This document contains public domain or Creative Commons (http://creativecommons.org) sites in the areas of audio/sound, music, clip art, video clips, photographs, and maps. Creation of the Film Festival Resource Guide was started by members of the instructional technology team who contributed resources that worked well with students and digital stories. Other members of the team reviewed the resources to verify the terms of use and licensing agreements, and once the sites were accepted, they were added to the resource list and reposted to the film website on the Copyright Free Resources page at www.pkwy.k12.mo.us/tis/filmfestival/copyright.cfm.

Limiting the Palette

Teachers often organize their own online libraries from which students may choose what they need to create their stories and have in-depth conversations with students about their projects so that they know what students are thinking as they write their scripts. Teachers then create folders on a network drive that contains media for student projects (music for creating mood, sound effects, possible clip art, and photographs). This type of classroom online library is generally used to enhance the live action footage that students have previously recorded. While setting up an online classroom library requires additional preparation from teachers, it also allows for a more suitable project timeline if time constraints are an issue. Students may only use items housed in their classroom library to enhance their projects. While this is more limiting than ranging freely through the Internet, it eliminates the possibility of students using copyrighted materials.

Using Google Advanced Search

Students always ask, "But can't we just use Google?" The answer is, "Sort of." While the following is not our preferred method, it's one that many teachers in our district use:

- Go to www.google.com and type in your keyword search.

- On the results page, click on Options cog wheel in the upper right and choose Advanced search.

- Click on the "usage rights" drop-down menu at the bottom left.

- Select the appropriate usage terms. For digital project, use "free to use or share."

- Click the Advanced search button, and a list of pictures and websites will show up in the results. Choose the "Images" link at the top to see only images.

- Many tiled images will display with links to any one of these. (Some could be blocked by a school network.)

- Search the site to see what the license restrictions are on that image.

- If the image can legitimately be used in digital projects, locate the author for use in citations credit.

Conversations on Copyright

Dialogue between teachers and students should focus on what it means to be a content creator. This will include how to find and use images and other resources respectfully. Through this process it's important to discuss and learn copyright vocabulary. While not an exhaustive list, we tend to focus on four basic terms when discussing ownership.

Public domain sources are the least restrictive and do not require providing attribution, but we highly recommend it. For example: http://ushistoryimages.com.

Attribution. Sources that ask for attribution need to include more traditional citations, such as the artist's name or screen name displayed on a credits page or near the image itself.

- The Stock.xchng (http://sxc.hu), a site with free stock photos, allows for filtering by license in the advanced search field.

- Wikimedia Commons (http://commons.wikimedia.org/wiki/Main_Page) includes a variety of images with detailed information on whether the photo needs a credit line (attribution) or not.

Creative Commons is a licensing organization allowing for a variety of different types of licenses. Media labeled "CC" will have more information about the terms for the artist's work. For more information visit http://creativecommons.org.

The GNU General Pubic License (GPL) is a free, copyleft license for software and other kinds of works (www.gnu.org/copyleft/gpl.html). It is usually accompanied by some information that will explain how the media can be used.

When searching and using sites for images and other media, beware that many sites are sponsored by for-profit companies. Sites such as iStockPhoto or Dreamstime offer photos that are *royalty-free* and *should not* be used without paying for them. Royalty-free does not mean "free"; it means "you only have to pay once," and then the image can be used as many times as needed.

Obtaining Permissions

One way to approach copyright is by simply asking the rights holder for permission to use the materials. This is an excellent lesson for students as they are beginning to think about ownership. In our film festival, we require written permission from each student artist, in the form of a letter or an email, that gives permission for that media to be used in *all* of the venues where that film will be shown. We also require students to give attributions in their credits to all sources.

> **TIP**
>
> The fastest and easiest way to find Creative Commons materials is to use the Creative Commons search engine on its site (http://search.creativecommons.org). Alternatively, include the term "creative commons" in the search query on any search site on the Internet.

Creating Original Pieces

As often as possible, we encourage students to create their own media for use in their projects. This ranges from using a camera to capturing still images or video to using loop-based music programs to creating original music. Through this process, students have a greater sense of ownership of their work as well as a sense of what it means to be a content creator.

Student Writing: Finding Clarity

As writers write, they discover their own understandings of their chosen topics. The same holds true in the creation of video. The process becomes one of discovery as filmmakers express themselves and take ownership of their stories. In all content areas, students are expected to have a certain mastery over the concepts they are studying. We want them to find connections between the content and their lives. When storytelling based on students' experiences is included in the classroom, students have a different relationship with the content. They are no longer consumers of a story that they may or may not care about; instead, they are creators of a version of a text or a concept that is a reflection of them. Through the creation process, they take ownership of their learning and understanding of the concepts involved in telling the story and creating the video.

When a new concept is first introduced to a student, the understanding of that concept is the teacher's. Right or wrong, biased or unbiased, the teacher owns the content, and students are "borrowing" it from him or her. As students begin to work through the lesson's activities, they begin to start making meaning; that is, they begin to understand the concept by associating it with their previous knowledge and experiences. At this point, the transfer of ownership of knowledge begins to shift from teacher to students. Students discover their own understandings of new concepts by building on the teacher's explanations and illustrations. Only when students are given opportunities to make their own meanings can they take owner-ship of ideas. The process of creating is a key element of this process. As students work through the material in order to create something original, they can't help but take ownership, thereby gaining a deeper under-standing of the concept.

Take, for example, Gina. Gina is an eighth grade student who is reading *The Outsiders*, a novel by S. E. Hinton, in her Communication Arts class. She read the book and understands the plot, but she has no ownership of the content.

Gina has borrowed her understanding of theme and conflict from her teacher and can pass any test on the book. However, for this class, there's no test, at least not in the traditional form. This time, Gina will be assessed on her understanding and interpretation of the concept and the story's themes. She and a small group of her classmates begin to explore the differences and similarities between "greasers" and "socs" and take their first steps as storytellers by starting to outline a script for a video. Soon they are filming and finally editing and producing. Through this process, Gina's understanding of the dynamics between these two fictional social groups continued to blossom. No longer did she need to rely on her teacher's interpretation of the text; she was drawing her own conclusions and making the story her own. At this point, regardless of the outcome of the final product, Gina has a different relationship with the book and the characters and a different understanding of the story. She is now a creator—a producer of content inspired by an external source and a generator of her own knowledge. Through the process, she has taken ownership of her own learning.

Gina and her classmates created a video called *The Outsider Jeans*, which can be seen at www.pkwy.k12.mo.us/pdmedia/?uuid=242. In this insightful video, the students' blue jeans are the characters. The actors' faces are never shown, and the sense of anonymity of the two groups shows the student filmmaker's understanding of the content. Gina's understanding is not borrowed but is deeply owned and understood. Instead of the paper and pencil test that she expected, Gina had to analyze, interpret, collaborate, and compromise. Not only that, her assessment gave her an audience outside the four walls of her teacher's classroom. *The Outsiders* became part of her, not just a book that she read one time in middle school.

While this kind of understanding won't happen in every instance, with every student, and every project, it wouldn't have happened at all without Gina being given the opportunity to create. Sometimes projects will end up being little more than advanced book reports. However, only through the opportunity to make meaning can students take ownership of ideas.

Production: *The Story Continues*

Once students complete the writing and storyboard process, they are ready to transfer the meaning of the content into video. This requires time, patience, and creativity. In order to foster time and patience, it is beneficial to provide mini lessons on filming, sound, lighting, and voice. Addressing these issues before filming will save time and ease frustrations during postproduction editing. It is easier to be proactive with filming than to be reactive after filming has occurred. Creativity in moviemaking is not typically taught in classrooms, but various moviemaking techniques should be.

Talking to students about ways to keep the audience engaged is also significant in creating a high-quality video. Too often, when students are handed a camera, audience and story are forgotten. During the production process, it's important to keep coming back to these elements and asking questions and reflecting on whether a certain shot moves the story along or if it stifles it. Another question to ask is whether the audience will be able to understand what a specific action conveys about the story or what the message from a specific scene or sequence is. While the focus of the next few pages is on technical elements and techniques, the conversations teachers and students should have must still clarify what the audience will understand and the purpose of each scene toward moving the story along.

What follows are considerations and possible mini lesson topics as students begin the production process. If they've planned well, they will have scripts and storyboards to follow, but don't assume that these technical elements come naturally to students.

Filming

- If students use their own video cameras, be sure to know what video format each camera produces. If the video format is not compatible with available software, the video will need to be converted before editing.

- Before and after filming the shot, leave three to five seconds of blank footage, so that when students edit, words and scenes don't get cut off.

- Use a tripod whenever possible; students are never as steady as they think they are when using hand-held cameras. If no tripod is available, lean the camera against a sturdy object and brace the camera firmly.

- To create different perspectives, shoot footage from different angles. This is a great way to infuse creativity and originality into the production.

- Avoid the "talking head" scene, unless it is crucial to the storyline.

- Check to see that all shots are clearly focused and framed. Check to see what is in the background of the scene.

- Close-ups are used to focus attention when necessary to illustrate a point and should be slow and steady.

- When panning a scene, be sure to use a tripod so that the scene remains smooth.

Sound

- Microphones can be good and bad depending on the taping environment. Microphones will pick up background noise that may not be suitable for the story. For example, a history project is set in the 1700s, and the audience hears or sees a trash truck pass by in the background of the scene. On the other hand, microphones work great for keeping voices at the desired volume.

- Try to keep background noises to a minimum. For example, it is not a good idea to tape when students are changing classes or in a classroom with other students working.

- Filming outside can be extremely challenging because sounds can be greatly distorted by even a gentle breeze.

Lighting

- Don't point the camera directly into the sun; if you do, the actors will be shadow images.

- On a similar note, avoid filming in shadows or partial light. Lighting changes can create unfocused shots.

- If filming inside, additional lighting maybe required to see all actions in a scene.

Voice and Actors

- Rehearse, rehearse, rehearse! The lines need to *feel* natural and not sound as if they're being read from a script.

- Actors knowing their lines will cut down on having to sift through footage that is not usable. Keeping notes as to which was the best take will also help speed up editing.

- Cue cards are great alternatives to memorization or reading directly from the script.

- Students need to talk clearly with good diction, keep volume consistent, and include voice inflections.

Saving Project Files

- Always have students upload new footage to a flash, network, or external drive, especially if the whole school is sharing the cameras. Another idea is for the teacher to keep a copy of all footage recorded in case something happens to the student's copy. Reshooting can eat up a lot of valuable time.

Using Production-Quality Images

In all cases, the images (video or still) that are part of the final product should directly link to the storyboard and should adhere to the following standards:

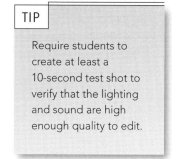

TIP

Require students to create at least a 10-second test shot to verify that the lighting and sound are high enough quality to edit.

- Graphics, photographs, and animations enrich the spoken or written theme.

- Images enhance rather than detract from the impact of the overall message in the story.

- Main points are explained and reinforced by image selection.

Postproduction: *The Story Comes Alive*

Once all footage is captured, it's time to take it to the cutting room and begin to edit everything together. There are many video-editing solutions available for both PC and Mac. Movie Maker and iMovie come free with their respective operating systems but can be somewhat limiting. There are many Web 2.0 tools or downloadable editing programs (including YouTube, Overstream, WeVideo and MovieMasher) that are either free or inexpensive and may do the job. There are also more professional tools, such as Adobe Premiere, Pinnacle Studio, and Final Cut Pro, which provide a wider variety of options, filters, and motion controls. Each of these programs offers a higher level of control over the finished product, but none are as intuitive as the free choices.

Authentic Voice: Clarity of Self

Even more interesting, as students begin to organize their stories, patterns begin to emerge in their storytelling methods. They have been influenced by their culture and by their experiences with media. Theirs is a culture of remixes, where content builds on other content and creation is inspired by what has already been created. In a classroom, it could be deemed cheating; in the real world, it's a source of inspiration. They are stirred by the media that they are bombarded with, and so, almost in tribute, they create and publish their own renditions of what they see, copying storylines and visual and audio techniques and methods. In so doing, they learn the advantages and limitations of the tools they are working with and become more and more adept. They aren't in awe of the technology that helps them create. Instead, they are in awe of what they can create with that technology.

There are many examples online of students' inspiration from music videos to entire projects completely based on the work of others. In 2011, Bill received an email from a friend whose daughter, Ana, was inspired by one of the promotional videos that students created for our film festival (www.pkwy.k12.mo.us/pdmedia/?uuid=C44DB1F7-1CC4-EACA-CE7F68C7624188C6).

The video that inspired Ana was created by a group of our high school art students who had recorded themselves drawing our film festival logo. The original video was 8 hours long, but in the end, they sped that up to 90 seconds, and the results were fantastic. Ana, a fifth grader, had seen the video from two states away and was inspired by it. She was fascinated with the technique and wanted to try it, so she videotaped herself making a Valentine's day box and sped up her video. It was a tribute to technique rather than story, but ultimately it was a reflection of her being inspired by others. Ana's video can be seen at www.youtu.be/s7gpL4osuUs.

Regardless of the software package, the focus needs to remain on the story that is being told, and the script and storyboards should be on hand as reference guides. One caution about the editing process: it's easy for students (and teachers alike) to get caught up in all the bells and whistles that come with these programs. Transitions, sound effects, and video filters have the potential to greatly enhance a film, but they can become exceedingly distracting to the viewer. These tools should only be used as a way to enhance or add meaning to the story. If these elements don't somehow add to the project, they shouldn't be used. This is an excellent opportunity to practice restraint and once again focus on the story.

In this final stage of the filmmaking process, as all the elements are put together, many technical pieces must be addressed. This is also where much of the frustration and angst about creating films with students comes into play. As we have helped students with their creations, we've helped them think about the process by making the connections to the order of operations protocol from math class. This strategy helps students with mechanics and time management, while easing frustration and making the process more efficient. This is also a good time to remind students of the curriculum goal of the production, to take time to review the rubric, and to refocus students on audience and purpose. Our adapted protocol from postproduction follows the following steps: gathering, editing, exporting, and publishing.

Gathering Files

Importing footage into the editing software requires the user to transfer the footage from the camera to a secure destination. Place all the captured video files for a film into a single folder, and place this folder in a location where students will not need to move it for the duration of the project. This is extremely important once the editing begins because the software links to these files as they are manipulated on the timeline. Changing or moving the original files will cause the link to be broken, removing those files from the project. Consider the following about film quality:

- The greater the quality and resolution of the captured material, the larger the size of the files involved.

- High-quality video takes up a huge amount of space, as much as 100+ megs per minute.

- Always refer back to the final audience and method of viewing. The highest quality capture is important if films are going to be shown on a very large screen.

- Standard definition capture is appropriate for most other situations. Just remember, the quality of the video can be decreased during the final export of the film, but at no time can quality be increased.

Editing

During the editing process, all elements of the final film (raw video, sound, and images) will be put together in one final project. Strategies such as limiting the palette (providing students with a limited set of resources such as sound effects and images) can be used in this process. At this stage, there is another opportunity to assess students on their editing skills, however, editing should be more about the process than a specific deliverable.

1. **Import clips.** Import/convert all video clips/pictures to the appropriate format depending on the editing software. Not all software supports all types of video, audio, and image formats, so it's important to test media before the project begins.

2. **Edit clips.** Edit the clips by splicing, trimming, and ordering the media, using the software (remind students to keep their original clips in a safe place and work from a copy).

3. **Transitions and effects.** These tools allow students to emphasize a particular scene, set the mood or feel of the video, or enhance the video in ways that cannot be captured during filming.

    - Adding an effect will change the appearance of the clip, so previewing the options and deciding how an effect will add rather than detract from a particular clip might be a good mini-lesson to have with students.

    - Transitions between scenes link words and actions together in a coherent fashion and keep the pace of the film moving forward. Keep them consistent and simple throughout the film.

4. **Titles.** Use easy-to-read fonts and avoid placing text over the subject of the scene.

5. **Sound.** Normalize sound to be as close to the same volume all the way through.

Consider the following about the editing process:

- Only the highest quality shots are kept and refined.

- Transitions are used in a mindful way to create a smooth, shot-to-shot flow within the story.

- The selection of effects supports appropriate emphasis in communicating the main idea.

- Encourage clips to be refined to emphasize action, and remove dead time to keep the story tempo moving.

- Sequence matters.

- Long clips without any dialogue or sound are very boring.

- Title pages can be strategically placed throughout the video to help ensure that sufficient information is provided.

- Have students ask themselves, "So what?" to make sure that everything included is really essential, not just cool or funny.

Another important part of the editing process is saving the project. For the most part, video projects (and editing specifically) will take place over a few days. This necessitates saving the project file to be worked on later. Regardless of the software system, a project file will be created, allowing students to go back in and continue editing at a later time. When we have students set up their projects, we have them store all of their media in one folder.

Figure 8.1 A student edits her digital film.

That same folder is where they will also save their project files so that, if need be, a project can be backed up or moved to a different computer by simply copying the entire folder to removable storage and copying it to a new computer. This is a key point that has saved countless projects over the years. However, this version of the project is not the final film. All of these files must now be exported into one single file that can then be submitted to the film festival.

Exporting the Project

Once all the files are edited and have been previewed for continuity and story, it's time to export the final project and publish the film. The final export process (also called rendering) will create a file that can be viewed with a multimedia player on a variety of different computers. To determine what resolution and quality are necessary depends on the final audience and method of viewing. With so many formats and software available, we cannot do justice to exact methods, but here are some rendering details to take into account when looking at the export settings:

Video Settings

- Movies that will be played in an online environment should use the 640 × 480 setting with a playback rate between 100 and 250 kbs (kilobytes per second).

- Movies being played on a TV or with a projector on a standard size screen benefit from higher resolution, say 1024 × 768, and a playback rate closer to 1–2 mbs (megabytes per second).

- The higher the playback rate, the better the quality of the video, but a high playback rate increases the file size drastically.

- Remember never to set the final export settings to a higher level than the original material as distortion will occur in the final project.

Audio Settings

- For audio quality, typically you'll choose from mono (one speaker) or stereo (dual speakers) sound, and playback quality rates from 11 khz up to 48 khz.

- For small screen playback, 22 khz will suffice, while 44 khz should be used for the big screen because audio is an important piece of the viewers' experience.

Once everything is set, export the video. It will take time to render the final product, as the software has to crunch the clips, effects, and audio together to the resolution and playback levels defined by the settings. The whole process is an act of patience and experimentation. Sometimes the chosen settings don't render out as planned. In these cases, changing settings to get the desired quality will take time, but the final result will be a source of pride for students. Depending on the output quality and number of additional elements, like transitions and effects, rendering time may vary widely. Be sure to build in rendering time for the computer to process the video. As a rough guideline, count on from two to four times a video's actual playing time for rendering. Students don't have to attend to the project during this time, but be sure to set aside time for rendering as project timelines are planned.

Publishing

Traditionally in education, students would create a project, turn it in to their teacher, and that would be the end of the process. In the digital age, many other venues for published work are available to students, which encourages them to create for a purpose and revise with a vision in mind. For example, students can publish work on YouTube, Google Drive, Dailymotion, Vimeo, or SchoolTube. Even though some of your students may already be publishing their videos on the Internet, publishing needs to become an integral part of classroom work, as it brings the entire creation process full circle. It's no longer enough for students to have teachers as their only audience.

As we have frequently stated in previous chapters, the ability to share videos online has changed the relationship between students and their creations. When students are creating for the world, their work will be *good*, and when they are creating only for their teachers, it will be *good enough* to get a grade. A better alternative for classroom projects is publishing work publicly because it changes the stakes of the creation and will change the creation process. Students no longer need to create simply because their teachers told them to. An assignment from a teacher may be the impetus to get them started, but ultimately, they will create videos for each other. The ease of publishing their work online and the importance of sharing that work with others are the strongest motivators for the movie-making process and, in the end, were the reasons why we created our film festival.

Movie Reflections

Once the project is completed or at the end of each stage of the video process, teachers should ask students to assess what they have learned through reflection, whether by means of an online forum, in a blog post, or as part of an ongoing wiki project. Reflection supports personal growth and encourages students to engage in a thoughtful inventory: taking account of what they already knew, what they learned through curriculum instruction, ways the project helped them make connections to their everyday lives, and how they value the overall educational merits of their projects. The process of reflection allows them not only to look at the process of creating movies, but also to understand the overall experience of creating, including justifying the decision of topic selection, analyzing all the parts of the topic, applying the researched information in new ways, and being able to explain the concepts to an audience via their original stories as videotaped. Similar to any other part of this process, the teacher will need to guide reflection time to help students derive meanings from their work.

The possibilities for questions that can be asked are endless and, many times, dependent upon the unit of study. However, throughout the creation process, students are asked to make decisions to tell their stories and to complete their videos most effectively. These decisions can be grouped into one of two categories, process or content, and both of these should be addressed during reflection time. When asking students to reflect upon the process, the following question prompts will help them analyze their creations:

- What transitions or video effects did you use in your movie? How did they add to the meaning behind your story?

- How did the music or soundtrack affect the message of your film?

- Pick one scene in your movie. Describe the scene, including the action and camera angles. Why did you choose to frame the image the way you did?

- What did you cut out of your film to meet the time limit requirements? How would that clip that was left out have added to your film if you could have kept it?

- What would you do differently if you were creating this project again?

- What do you feel is the best scene in your film and why?

Each of these questions requires students to think about their creation process and analyze the decisions they made in the creation process. While some of them overlap with the content category, having students answer these questions gets to the heart of the decisions that they had to make. The fourth question in this list (about the clip that had to be cut) is especially important because it makes students think beyond the final product and asks them to predict a different outcome.

Questions in the content category are far more dependent upon the unit of study, in that the goals and outcomes for the unit should be reflected in the final work. However, students can still be asked to analyze their learning through reflective responses. This can be done by analyzing their own projects, but it may also be accomplished by having them analyze each other's projects to look for inconsistencies in content or different ways of explaining or telling their stories. This type of reflection is especially powerful when students realize that they are learning to see the world from points of view that are different from their own.

CHAPTER **9**

Curriculum and Assessment

In order to create a digital project that reflects transfer of knowledge, attention must be given to the desired results, formative/summative assessment evidence, and learning experiences. Higher quality projects will evolve when it has been decided what students should be able to do with acquired content and when rubrics have been created that define expectations. Video creation should be more than simply presenting information. Use it as a tool to evoke emotions that encourage discussion, create awareness, and awaken curiosity about important topics and concepts.

Digital projects will look different across various content areas. In a communication arts class, many of the projects are based on writing units; therefore, telling stories in different genres may come naturally. When working in other content areas that showcase nonfiction, the focus is on answering an interesting question in a way that drives a story forward yet does more than report the facts.

The writing process in all content areas encourages students to use sensory details, feelings, and thoughts, thereby increasing the rigor of studying a particular topic and causing students to think more deeply about fundamental ideas. Benchmarks, such as local/state standards, NETS•S standards, and 21st-century learning will also impact curriculum planning. Luckily, there is a correlation between the NETS•S competencies and the 21st-century cluster of skills that can work together with desired unit objectives to create a platform for more meaningful projects. To ensure desired results, one suggestion might be to scaffold each stage of the project by implementing formative assessments that require students to meet progress expectations before going to the next stage. Reflecting on the final product with content and digital storytelling rubrics are summative assessment tools.

ISTE's NETS Standards

ISTE's NETS have been a driving force in the creation of our festival. We wanted to be sure that students and teachers were meeting not only state curricular standards, but also the technology standards that would help move us forward as a district as we strive to integrate more technology into classrooms. We identified the following NETS standards for students, teachers, administrators, and coaches as ones that would align with the film estival project. (See Appendix B for the NETS in their entirety.)

NETS•S

1. Creativity and Innovation
2. Communication and Collaboration
3. Research and Information Fluency
4. Critical Thinking, Problem Solving, and Decision Making
5. Digital Citizenship
6. Technology Operations and Concepts

NETS•T

1. Facilitate and Inspire Student Learning and Creativity

2. Design and Develop Digital-Age Learning Experiences and Assessments

3. Model Digital-Age Work and Learning

4. Promote and Model Digital Citizenship and Responsibility

NETS•A

1. Visionary Leadership

2. Digital-Age Learning Culture

3. Excellence in Professional Practice

NETS•C

1. Visionary Leadership

2. Teaching, Learning, and Assessments

3. Digital-Age Learning Environments

4. Professional Development and Program Evaluation

5. Digital Citizenship

6. Content Knowledge and Professional Growth

Framework for 21st-Century Learning

The Partnership for 21st Century Skills (www.p21.org) is a national organization that advocates for the 4Cs (critical thinking, communication, collaboration, and creativity) in addition to the 3Rs within our schools to better prepare students for the demands of digital age innovation. Through the film festival process, students are interacting with 21st-century skills by blending content knowledge with literacies that support multidimensional abilities. Digital storytelling supports the framework for 21st Century Student Outcomes in a variety of ways.

Table 9.1 Correlation of 21st Century Skills to Digital Storytelling

21st Century Student Outcomes	Digital Storytelling
Core Subjects 3Rs & 21st Century Themes (global awareness; financial, economic, business, and entrepreneurial literacy; civic, health, and environmental literacy)	Digital storytelling requires students to master core subjects and understand academic content at transformational levels.
Learning & Innovative Skills—4Cs (critical thinking, communication, collaboration, and creativity)	Digital storytelling involves students acting on creative ideas, using systems thinking, and collaborating effectively to solve unfamiliar problems.
Information, Media, & Technology Skills	Digital storytelling leads students to utilize rapidly changing technology tools, assess information accurately, and apply digital craftsmanship.
Life & Career Skills	Digital storytelling allows students to adapt to change, be productive and accountable members of a team, and act responsibly to accomplish a common goal.

Source for left column: Partnership for 21st Century Skills, www.p21.org.

Formative Assessments: Creating Video

In the *Journal of Computing in Teacher Education*, Erica R. Halverson and Damiana Gibbons (2010) identify some key areas where formative assessments can occur in the process of creating digital videos. We have adapted what these authors call "key moments as pedagogical windows" for use with our teachers. We are not skipping the filming process in these four key areas; rather, we are assuming that these steps will be completed before the editing can begin. The four key areas are the pitch, storyboarding, editing, and public presentation.

The Pitch

This is the point at which students present their ideas about their story to their teacher. It's the moment where "youth demonstrate what they have learned so far about storytelling and what they plan to do in the next stages in the process" (Halverson & Gibbons, 2010). Additionally, the presentation of ideas provides insights into the students' understanding and tells the teacher what more they will need to be taught to make their visions a reality. This additional learning can include storytelling and film techniques as well as organizational structure and planning.

Form 9.1 (page 130) provides sample questions for assessing the pitch.

Storyboarding

To find success, students must develop a plan for their filming. At this moment, the teacher can teach or reteach storytelling concepts, address flow, and work on technical aspects of filmmaking. We encourage teachers to have students create a complete set of storyboards, using traditional methods, such as notecards and paper templates, as well as presentation tools like PowerPoint and Keynote. They can then print out and mark up their storyboards as needed.

TIP

Giving students a digital camera to create visuals for shots when story-boarding gives them the opportunity to think inside a frame and see what the camera will actually see.

Form 9.2 is a sample guide meant to give feedback to students around their planning process. Using this as a formative assessment will help guide students with their planning and make the filming process go more smoothly.

Form 9.1 Questions to Assess the Pitch

What is the purpose of your story? (i.e., instructional, informational, documentary, persuasive, story).	☐ Clear Understanding ☐ Vague Understanding ☐ Still Developing Ideas
Notes:	

What is your message?	☐ Clear Understanding ☐ Vague Understanding ☐ Still Developing Ideas
Notes:	

Who is your audience?	☐ Clear Understanding ☐ Vague Understanding ☐ Still Developing Ideas
Notes:	

What is your vision for the beginning, middle, and end of your story?	☐ Clear Understanding ☐ Vague Understanding ☐ Still Developing Ideas
Notes:	

Who are your characters, and what is your setting?	☐ Clear Understanding ☐ Vague Understanding ☐ Still Developing Ideas
Notes:	

What medium do you plan to use? (e.g., still photos, video, animation)	☐ Clear Understanding ☐ Vague Understanding ☐ Still Developing Ideas
Notes:	

What questions do you have before you can move forward?

Form 9.2 Storyboard Assessment

Category: Writing		
The story is easy to follow and shows significant planning.		
Strong	Some	Limited
Evidence of solid planning: clearly moves from part to part in a well-thought-out manner.	Evidence of planning but transition of events needs more work.	Story is confusing, and the purpose is not present.
Notes:		

Category: Structure		
The story is told with the right number of key details for the audience to follow along with the story.		
Strong	Some	Limited
Story flows naturally because it is told with the right number of details.	Story has inconsistent flow; it may need more or fewer details.	Story has choppy flow; there are too few or too many details. Story needs extensive editing.
Notes:		

Category: Organization		
Events and messages are presented in a logical order.		
Strong	Some	Limited
Storyline is well-developed and contains a beginning, middle, and end with a target audience in mind.	Storyline contains a purpose, but elements of the story are missing.	Storyline is difficult to follow or does not exist.
Notes:		

(Continued)

Form 9.2 Storyboard Assessment *(Continued)*

Category: Media

The media supports the story.

Strong	Some	Limited
Images and sounds create a distinct tone to symbolize or enrich emotion that complements the story.	Images and sounds need editing in order to support the story.	Images and sounds do not match the story.

Notes:

Category: Resources

There is a plan for locating safe and appropriate media in respect to copyright.

Strong	Some	Limited
Resources for information are well documented; participants are identified consistently.	Resources for information are mostly documented; identification of participants may be incomplete.	Documentation of resources is weak or missing; participants are not identified.

Notes:

Category: Group Work (if applicable)

There is a plan that identifies the role of each participant.

Strong	Some	Limited
Each person in the group has an identified role and knows what his/her responsibility is within the project.	Roles and responsibilities need further refinement among group members.	Roles are undefined, and responsibilities have not been delegated.

Notes:

Editing

Assessing editing is a little different from the other key areas because there is no deliverable product that can be identified. Rather, in this process, "learning is demonstrated through dialogue about how a piece should evolve" (Halverson & Gibbons, 2010). All learning up to this point comes together when the writer/ storyteller and editors (peers as well as the teacher can act as editors) have a dialogue about the application of tools, storytelling, and understanding of concept. This becomes a time of discovery, when students can help each other actually to create and mold their understanding; through this process, they take ownership of ideas, story, and knowledge. Editing can look very different from classroom to classroom. The key is to conduct conversations with students about their process and what they have created and to encourage them to edit each other's work. Hundreds of decisions are made in the editing process. Through conversations about why students chose to make particular decisions, teachers can assess the learning as students analyze their own work. This helps ensure that the message of the project helps to define each student's understanding of the concept being taught. Form 9.3 is a sample for guiding those conversations with students.

Form 9.3 Questions to Assess the Editing Process

What emotion, awareness, or curiosity was conveyed to the audience?	☐ Clear Understanding ☐ Vague Understanding ☐ Still Developing Ideas
Notes:	
How does the selection of video content (images and sound) enhance the message of your story?	☐ Clear Understanding ☐ Vague Understanding ☐ Still Developing Ideas
Notes:	
Explain two decisions that you made in the editing process that were important to the story and why you made them.	☐ Clear Understanding ☐ Vague Understanding ☐ Still Developing Ideas
Notes:	
What questions do you have before you can move forward?	

Public Presentation

Through publishing their projects (entering videos in the film festival), students complete a performance event for an authentic audience and demonstrate their knowledge through their interpretation of the curricular materials. Prior to the screening of their videos, the final piece of the creation process, students should be invited to reflect on both their work and their learning.

Form 9.4 Sample Reflection Questions for Public Presentation

- What transitions or video effects did you use in your movie? How did they add to the meaning behind your story?

- What did the music or soundtrack add to the message of your film? How did you want it to affect the audience's reaction to your film?

- Pick one scene in your movie. Describe the scene, including the action and camera angles. Why did you choose to frame the image the way you did?

- What did you cut out of your film to meet the time limit requirements? How would that cut clip have added to your film if you could have kept it?

- What would you do differently if you were creating this project again?

- What do you feel is the best scene in your film and why?

- What makes your story original or unique?

- What reaction to the story do you want your audience to have?

- What did you learn from viewing other students' projects?

- How did your story demonstrate what you have learned?

Teachers can ask students to think about what they have learned while they are watching their videos at the film festival. If this reflection is missing from the process, learning goals may be lost amid the bells and whistles that can overwhelm the creation process and take focus away from the goals. As mentioned in Chapter 8, this reflective practice helps students define what they have learned and analyze the decisions they made throughout the process. Reflection can be done in many ways after the videos are screened as well, via a blog post, a paper, or even a conversation. It is important that time be given to students to reflect on their own learning.

Throughout the creation process, we encourage teachers to continue to have conversations with students so that these assessments can occur. It's easy for these reflection questions (especially the last two) to get lost in the struggle to complete projects, but they are important parts of the learning process.

Through observations and experiences of working with teachers, many times the formative assessment piece is not something that is done consciously; rather, it happens informally and not systematically. When this happens, students tend to get lost in the process due to time constraints; therefore, a more thoughtful, intentional approach is necessary. Assessment happens in various ways and at various times, sometimes tangible and other times not, but it is a transition that includes assorted methods of formative assessment, reflection, and a summative consideration, like a compendium of experiences between the written word and the visual experience.

The Importance of Summative Assessment

The ultimate idea behind assessment is having students decode their decisions for optimal learning to occur. Thinking critically about decisions they made and why they made them enhances the transfer of knowledge, from doing more than reporting on a topic to thinking more deeply about a fundamental idea.

After publishing their videos, students reflect on the final product in terms of content and the digital story. The final step is the summative assessment of the entire project and process. This assessment is meant to give students a final grade and is the culmination of the feedback and work they have done throughout the project.

The following rubric is meant to be a starting point for teachers as they create their own rubrics, customized to meet the curricular goals of the project.

Form 9.5 Rubric for Published Digital Story

Planning			
Criteria	3 points	2 points	1 point
Writing: The story is easy to follow and shows significant planning.	Evidence of solid planning: clearly moves from part to part in a well-thought-out manner.	Evidence of planning but transition of events needs more work.	Story is confusing, and the purpose is not present.
Structure: The story is told with the right number of key details for the audience to follow along with the story.	Story flows naturally because it is told with the right number of details.	Story has inconsistent flow; it may need more or fewer details.	Story has choppy flow; there are too few or too many details. The story needs extensive editing.
Organization: Events and messages are presented in a logical order.	Storyline is well-developed and contains a begin-ning, middle, and end with a target audience in mind.	Storyline contains a purpose, but elements of the story are missing.	Storyline is difficult to follow or does not exist.
Evaluator's comments:			

Form 9.5 Rubric for Published Digital Story *(Continued)*

Use of Technology			
Criteria	3 points	2 points	1 point
Media: The media supports the story.	Images and sounds create a distinct tone to symbolize or enrich emotion that complements the story.	Images and sounds need editing in order to support the story.	Images and sounds do not match the story.
Editing: The edits help the story flow and do not distract from the story.	Transitions, effects, audio, and edits are appropriate to the message, add flow to the story, and most importantly, do not distract from the story.	Some transitions, effects, audio, and edits are appropriate to the message, add flow to the story, and most importantly, do not distract from the story.	Little to no transitions, effects, audio, and edits are appropriate to the message, add flow to the story, and most importantly, do not distract from the story.
Credits: Resources are copyright-friendly and appropriate.	Resources of information are well documented; participants are identified consistently.	Resources of information mostly documented; identification of participants may be incomplete.	Documentation of resources weak or missing; participants are not identified.
Evaluator's comments:			

(Continued)

Form 9.5 Rubric for Published Digital Story *(Continued)*

Group Work—If applicable			
Students use this section for self and peer evaluation			
Criteria	3 points	2 points	1 point
Participation: Work is equally distributed among the group members.	Work was completed equally by all group members.	Work was mostly completed by a portion of the group members.	Work was mostly completed by one group member.
Cooperation: Group members work cooperatively and treat each other with respect.	All participants respect each other's views and opinions.	Evidence of respect among group members is shown most of the time.	Lack of respect is evident in group interactions.
Evaluator's comments:			

CHAPTER 10

On the
Red Carpet

*The night of the film festival is an invaluable experience.
The most important piece of the entire event is
honoring students. One of the goals that we hold dear
is to make kids feel like rock stars. Through our
planning and preparation, we do just that.*

Orchestrating the Event

On the actual day of the festival, there is still much work to be done to make sure the event goes smoothly. If the planning up until now has been thorough, the event itself should go very well. There are really three areas to attend to, depending on the festival's scope: the auditorium, the control booth, and the lobby.

The Auditorium

The team leader is responsible for timing and making sure the festival runs smoothly; he or she will spend most of the night in the auditorium. Juggling communication with the technical and lobby teams and working with the emcee to be sure everything runs smoothly, the leader makes final decisions on when doors open and when the films actually start playing.

> **TIP**
>
> Without fail, something will go wrong. It's important to be flexible throughout the evening. Have fun!

Some festivals need to have ushers present if seating is at a premium for the venue. It's important that everyone enjoys the night, so be sure to make finding a seat a pleasant experience.

The overall timeline for the event may vary, but there are definitely some consistencies that every festival should have.

- **Welcome.** Be sure to welcome the audience to the festival, and clearly state its purpose and academic rationale. It's important for everyone to understand that learning and education are at the heart of every film.

- **Intermission.** Most festivals will need an intermission. Audience members will need to have some sort of break if there are a large number of films.

- **Closing.** Unlike a typical movie, the end of the festival is an opportunity to thank attendees both for making the films and for coming to the event. Also, take this opportunity to once again make a connection between the filmmaking process and the education of the students involved. While this may seem excessive, it helps to drive home the purpose behind the event.

Some optional items:

- **Raffle.** If sponsors have donated items for a raffle, intermission is a perfect time to draw student names. Since we don't choose a "best picture," these items are not awards but are participation prizes. All students who participate in the festival have their names entered into a drawing once and the emcee pulls the names announcing them live at the event. In the past, we have given away video cameras, laptops, game consoles, and other items. It's not a crucial part of the night but does help motivate participation and creates excitement for attendees.

- **Special recognition.** There may be people in the audience who need to be recognized for their contributions. In our festival, we only take time to recognize students in a formal way. Because it's such a big part of our marketing, we formally recognize the students who created the film festival posters and present them with a framed copy of their poster. Sponsors and partners are graciously recognized in the festival program, during the intermission at the raffle, and in the lobby/atrium decorations.

The Control Booth

The control booth is where the technical aspects of the festival take place. It is where the computer that holds films and audio is controlled. The team members who are manning this booth should be in constant contact with the team leader for timing cues and audio volume corrections. If the festival is being held in an auditorium equipped with a sound system and lighting, this is also where those elements are controlled. During our festival, the typical evening follows this general order.

1. Upon arrival, the technical team connects the computer where the final rendered file with the films in it is stored and tests screen and audio quality to make sure nothing has changed since the dress rehearsal a few days earlier.

2. When the emcee arrives, a microphone check is done, and the stage spotlight is set. Lighting levels are then checked, and the script with each lighting and visual cue for the evening is double checked so everyone knows what is happening and when.

3. Once all these checks are complete, the film festival logo is displayed on the screen, and student-created music is played in the auditorium. At this point, the doors are opened, and families are allowed to find their seats.

4. For approximately 30 minutes before show time, two different items are shown on the screen. The first image is simply the logo. It should be a big part of the branding of the festival and should become synonymous with the event itself. The other visual is a rolling credit screen that lists the names of all students and teachers who have participated by submitting a film. It also recognizes sponsors, administrators, and other student creators. These rolling credits are a favorite of students and families as they look for their names in the list.

5. Five minutes before show time, the lights dim to signify that the festival is about to start, and promotional videos are played, welcoming families to the festival.

6. When these promotional videos are finished, the emcee welcomes families to the festival and explains the purpose of the festival. At this time, the technical team is responsible for adjusting lighting and microphone levels.

7. Just before the festival films are shown, the logo comes up one last time and fades out to another screen that announces the elementary featured films.

8. For the first section of the night, the technical team is in constant communication with the team leader, checking on volume levels and generally making sure that nothing catastrophic happens.

9. Once the elementary section of the evening is over, there is a 15-minute intermission. This time mimics the beginning of the festival on the big screen with alternation of the credits and logo, culminating with the emcee returning to the stage.

For the technical team, their job for the evening is to make sure that all the films run and that the items that need to be on the screen are there. They are very much like the stage crew in a play. They are behind-the-scenes players who are waiting for cues from the team leader as the evening is orchestrated.

The Lobby

The lobby is where the atmosphere of the festival really gets started. Be sure that there are team members there to welcome families as they arrive. In our case, members of the Instructional Technology Department play this role. We've considered having students and teachers who submitted films be greeters, but we chose not to because we wanted them to be honored rather than having to work the event.

Figure 10.1 Walking the red carpet

These instructional technology (IT) team members help attendees understand the layout and time schedule for the evening. Families are then free to mill about the lobby, students can walk down the red carpet (Figure 10.1), and browse the On-Demand Film booths to watch any film that has been submitted to the festival.

On the red carpet, one team member should be there to announce students and their film's title over a sound system before they walk. This adds to the ambience of the event and calls even more attention to the students and their work. The red carpet is a favorite among attendees and parents. One thing that we've done with this is to allow any student who has submitted a film to walk on the red carpet. With their VIP badges as their ticket, students are given a lanyard when they arrive and are then given the VIP treatment for the rest of the night. A team member will need to be responsible for handing out the lanyards for students to clip to their VIP badges and organizing students to prepare for their turn on the red carpet.

One or two team members also need to be available to hand out programs as families enter the auditorium. We found that if we allowed families to take as many programs as they want, we quickly ran out, as many were taken for scrapbooks and other mementos. Finally, it's a good idea to have a team member who can float to wherever there is a need. This person also communicates with the team leader to be sure that everything runs smoothly and can fill in as needed.

Our choice is to do the red carpet extravaganza twice because we split the evening into elementary and secondary sections. Approximately five minutes into intermission, we begin to announce secondary students, providing enough time for everyone to be recognized before the films begin again.

It's hard to capture the excitement of the night in text. As we work to orchestrate the event itself, students and their families and friends mingle in the lobby, waiting for the doors to open. They gather around the On-Demand Films kiosks and watch the videos that they and their friends produced. Their names are announced as they walk down the red carpet to the cheers of the spectators flanking each side. It is a special night for them, one they won't soon forget, as they can share their experiences online by sending and posting links to their videos. Inside the auditorium, the air buzzes with anticipation and excitement as students see themselves larger than life on the screen. If all goes well, no one in the audience will know the preparations that went into bringing this night to fruition, but all will remember what it felt like to walk the red carpet.

CHAPTER 11

After the Lights Come Up

*As with any large-scale project, constant reflection is
required in order for it to succeed for any extended length
of time. Simply talking among our group provided
insights, but we desired input from multiple sources:
members of the educational technology community,
teachers, administrators, parents, students, and others.
Only with this level of feedback could we expect
the Parkway Digital Film Festival to evolve in
a meaningful way and for the better.*

Reflections and Feedback

Any reflection should be proportional to the scope of your festival. Reflection and feedback may, as in our case, yield unintended and unforeseen consequences for a film festival. We hope that sharing the situations we have encountered and our responses to those situations will be helpful to you as you plan your own film festivals.

Culture

Culture will dictate much of what a festival could become and how it might get there. Be ready for the expectations of peers and colleagues to come to the forefront. Inevitably, some will see this project as an incredible learning opportunity for students, while others will see an unbelievable waste of time. A way to approach this requires, in some instances, a different perspective. A film festival first and foremost, should be about students, but realistically, there is a much larger audience. Make the festival an event to be remembered with positive accomplishments in the areas of culture, pride, venue, marketing, assessment, function, and buy-in. As we began our festival, we found that many of the cultural challenges we faced were due to the fact that many of our teachers had never edited videos or thought about using them in their classrooms. By providing them support throughout the process, we lowered the barriers to entry and created starting points for them and their students.

Pride

The perception of a district, school, or classroom is important to consider. Because of the public nature of such an event, it's important to make it worthwhile and to represent each school and the district well. Just as with any activity, be sure that the public face is one of pride in the students who are being honored. How better to show them off than a film festival with media coverage, showcasing the amazing work being accomplished by students K–12 who are using a medium that is as current and relevant as it gets? Partnering with HEC-TV and involving the district's public relations department went a long way toward instilling pride in students, teachers, staff members, and administrators.

Venue

Whether your film festival is an event sponsored by a teacher at the classroom level or an administrator at the district level, the idea of a venue makes people notice. A classroom teacher might check out the building's theater, library, or atrium. A building administrator could try going to the high school theater or administration offices. For district level employees, try going off campus. Do whatever it takes to make students feel as if the festival is and they are important. Invite parents, other teachers, and siblings. Provide an audience that is authentic to the student in an environment that tells the students this is special. After a year or two, it may be necessary to go bigger.

Marketing

With as many things as there are to consider in an educational institution, it is easy for good ideas to become muddled and/or lost. Marketing sets an event above the rest. The best thing we did was create a unique and eye-catching logo to help brand ourselves. The logo is located on all of the literature we publish, both digitally and in print, and is a focal point around which all things are built. This is not to say the logo is the only method of marketing. Try looking for ways to incorporate students' many talents, such as having them create posters that will be made public. Encourage them to create a radio spot that could play on local radio. Create a festival song that plays on all commercials and at the event, much like the easily recognizable anthem for all 20th Century Fox movies. Whatever the methods, keep the festival idea at the forefront of peoples' minds, and provide a consistent, simple, and constant message. After a few years, significantly less work will be needed to promote your festival.

Assessment

It was very interesting for the Instructional Technology Department to see the wide variety of entries and what teachers considered exceptional video projects. In the infancy of the film festival, we were simply looking for videos to show. What we received demonstrated students' and teachers' abilities to use video as a legitimate classroom tool. Indirectly, we were able to assess whether the faculty as a whole was meaningfully integrating technology into existing curricula. The festival became a powerful tool that gives direction for the professional development our department provides to teachers. Ultimately, the use of video in the classroom changed the way some of our teachers approached the teaching profession. Creating videos is not a throwaway activity; it has become a meaningful part of their professional skill set and gives them a meaningful, authentic performance event as a way to assess students' learning.

Function

The function of a film festival will inevitably change over time, and many powers will need to be in force to cause this change. Do not be afraid of the change, but be prepared. As cultures, expectations, students, and administrations change, so will the event. For us, the first year was just to see whether a festival could happen. The novelty of a district-wide event, getting all the cogs to function together, and then actually receiving a set of videos to show and having people show up was exhilarating. For our first year, the focus was simply participation. As time passed, the novelty, both for the creators of the film festival and the district that supported it, faded to some extent.

Did this thing called the Parkway Digital Film Festival warrant the time, energy, and funds it was consuming? It became necessary to show how the work we were doing directly influenced the students in the classroom and enhanced the curriculum. Establishing the expectation that the submitting teachers must provide a curricular connection for all video entries helped to solidify the validity of the festival. During the second year, our attention turned to enhancing curriculum through better storytelling and encouraging stronger student voices. For years two and three, our focus was on the storytelling. We did not want every student to turn in a digital book report. Our hope was for more personal, meaningful content.

For the fourth and subsequent years, we hope to focus on stronger production quality while maintaining the high quality of stories. As teachers and students become more comfortable with the technology surrounding video creation, the content they create will become more complex. To foster this, additional professional development will be provided, focusing specifically on sound quality, chroma key and proper lighting techniques, as well as continuing our digital storytelling classes. Overall, we have concluded that while each year we are striving to build the best possible film festival for students, the emphasis of each festival will change, and there will always need to be a specific focus.

Buy-In

Be ready for the question, "How am I/are we supposed to accomplish this?" It could come from other teachers or possibly administrators. If participating in the festival is not easy and meaningful for teachers, it more than likely will not happen. To make things work for our staff and administration, we focused on the following issues for teachers and administrators.

Teachers

The position of the technology integration specialist (TIS) is designed to provide support for faculty and staff at every technological turn. Lesson planning with teachers and providing them a step-by-step model to create a movie, from brainstorming to storyboarding to rendering, removes many of the stresses that go with creating a project/event of this scope. Unfortunately, upon first go-around, there may not be much or any support, and in the immediate future all support for faculty members may fall to one or two organizers or tech specialists. Bring in experts. Perhaps district technology personnel, a literacy coach from the building, or an involved parent from an applicable field will be willing to help. There may even be student experts within the classroom. Once the projects are finished, the video submission process and the management of students' data must be streamlined. Provide participants with a central location where they can submit their work and a straightforward method for collecting student data. Try to remove as many burdens as possible from teachers, including following up.

Administrators

Most administrators who might consider creating or supporting a film festival may not realize that most of the work to be done by teachers will be beyond what they were doing when they were in the classroom. Access to computers and other sophisticated electronic devices has changed, technology is constantly changing, and, most importantly, students' expectations continue to change. Students and their capabilities are quite different from just five years ago. Students understand how to operate many devices with cameras and take for granted having 24/7 instant access to information and communications through the web. Many of our students already have the basic skills and technical expertise for video creation. However, what a film festival offers that is so powerful is a structured educational setting for significant creation and innovation.

Creating videos as part of the curriculum allows students to be honored in a different way. Students who are not high achievers yet are interested in technology and video become motivated, creative learners. To quote an administrator from our district, "[The film festival] is the best thing that Parkway does for students." Just as this project is good for kids, it is good for schools and districts. A film festival gives administrators a wide variety of positive work products they can take pride in. A film festival allows students to shine in innovative, diverse ways that have more lasting value to themselves and their teachers than scores on standardized tests or grade-point averages.

Keeping It Student Centered

Remember, this event is about students. Each year, it's important to find new ways to bring student work to the forefront. How can the talents of an increasing number of students be showcased in meaningful ways? Each year we have added a new element to the festival. During the fall semester, art students design posters that are displayed in every building in the district. These students are honored the night of the festival along with the student filmmakers. Student-created music is played during the intermission and in the lobby before and after the show. Jazz bands from different schools play while students walk the red carpet. Each addition functions as one more way to bring in more students, all of whom are honored as VIPs the night of the festival. Every creation of the festival is built by students; we simply provide a venue to showcase their talents.

Meeting Standards

Considering the sheer volume of material teachers are required to cover and the emphasis that is placed on standardized testing, teachers may find it difficult to devote class time to a large-scale, multidisciplinary project that will not be directly tested. However, the need for just such a project is paramount. Sir Ken Robinson said, "We are educating people out of their creative capacities. … We don't grow into creativity, we grow out of it, or rather we get educated out of it" (Robinson, 2006). Nevertheless, to get teachers to buy into scheduling time for student-created videos, they must see a direct linkage between curricular goals and standards and the meanings that students derive from this project.

To demonstrate the meaning and validity of video creation, one avenue to take is connecting to state and district standards. In general terms (using the language of Common Core Standards, as they "build upon strengths and lessons of current state standards"), a film festival provides the opportunity for students to "integrate knowledge and ideas, produce and distribute writing, present knowledge, and collaborate on and delineate between multiple ideas."

Specific National Educational Technology Standards for Students (NETS•S; see Appendix B) are addressed throughout the process of video creation. Some of the skills students develop that are directly related to educational technology standards, as defined by ISTE (2007), are the following.

Students:

- create original works as a means of personal or group expression (1b);

- contribute to project teams to produce original works or solve problems (2d);

- locate, organize, analyze, evaluate, synthesize, and ethically use information from a variety of sources and media (3b);

- plan and manage activities to develop a solution or complete a project (4b);

- advocate and practice safe, legal, and responsible use of information and technology (5a);

- select and use applications effectively and productively (6b).

Without a doubt, though the process of creating videos meets academic standards in myriad ways, the keys are to identify and elucidate those connections in ways that are acceptable to all. Videos definitely take time to create, and through that creative process, learning is present in every step.

Other Realities

Accurately assessing a team or district is the first hurdle when structuring a film festival. To do this effectively, build an in-depth understanding of the pertinent realities, including the following:

- **Copyright.** Where are the faculty and staff in terms of understanding copyright? If this is a classroom project, is everything fair game under the guise of fair use? If there is a broad audience, should careful attention be paid to what is acceptable and what is not?

- **Growth.** What if more videos come in or more teachers want to participate? How can the increased traffic of family, friends, and colleagues wanting to view films be handled? If films become more complicated, how can the production time frame be adjusted for students?

- **Access.** Is the proper equipment accessible? If not, how will equipment needs be met? What software is available to edit video? Are the hardware and software compatible? What publishing platform should be used? Is this platform accessible to a larger audience?

- **Professional Development.** If students do not know how to work with the tools, who teaches them? Who teaches the teachers? What types of classes and professional development need to be designed and initiated at the department/building/district level? Are classes enough? How can a teacher get in-class help, in regard to more hands-on assistance and instruction on more effective teaching practices? When things go wrong, who has the answers?

These are important questions that we cannot accurately answer for every teacher in every district, due to the unique nature of each classroom, building, and district. Throughout this book, we have addressed many of these questions as they apply to our district. If our approaches are viable for you, then by all means use, borrow, change, twist, and manipulate them. Please use this book as a guide to create a version of the Parkway Digital Film Festival that fits your district's goals. Students will appreciate the opportunities a film festival presents, and teachers will get immense satisfaction from watching students create connections between learning and self-expression through technology.

APPENDIX A

Online Resources

www.youtube.com

YouTube is a video-sharing website on which users can upload, share, and view videos. The service is used to display a wide variety of user-generated video content, including movie clips, TV clips, and music videos, as well as amateur content, such as video blogging and short original videos.

www.teachertube.com

TeacherTube is a video-sharing website similar to and based on YouTube. It is designed to allow those in the educational field, particularly teachers, to share educational resources, such as videos, audios, documents, photos, groups, and blogs. The site contains a mixture of classroom teaching resources and others designed to aid teacher training. A number of students have also uploaded videos that they have made as part of K–12 and college courses.

www.phpmotion.com

PHPmotion is a free-to-use, video-sharing, content management system written in PHP and using MySQL databases and FFmpeg. PHPmotion does not require payment to use, but a "Powered by PHPmotion" link is required unless a fee is paid. The software gives average persons the ability to have their own video-sharing website. PHPmotion supports many different video and audio formats that include MPG, AVI, DIVX, MP3 and WMA.

www.dropbox.com

Dropbox is a web-based, file-hosting service operated by Dropbox, Inc. that uses cloud computing to enable users to store and share files and folders with others across the Internet using file synchronization. There are both free and paid services, each with varying options. In comparison with similar services, Dropbox offers a relatively large number of user clients large amounts of storage space across a variety of desktop and mobile operating systems.

www.box.com

Box (formerly Box.net) is an online file-sharing network and cloud content management service for enterprise, business, and personal accounts. The company has adopted a "freemium" business model and provides 5GB of free storage for personal accounts. A mobile version of the service is available for iPhone, iPad, Android, and WebOS devices.

http://aws.amazon.com/s3

> **Amazon s3** or **Simple Storage Service** is an online storage web service offered by Amazon Web Services. Amazon s3 provides storage through web services interfaces (REST, SOAP, and BitTorrent). Pricing is based on tiers where end users storing more than 50 terabytes receive discounted pricing. Amazon claims that s3 uses the same scalable storage infrastructure that Amazon.com uses to run its own global e-commerce network.

www.flash-video-mx.com/flv_encoder_sdk

> **Flash Video MX SDK V2** is an on-demand solution "to convert video to Flash within a COM and Flash Video MX SDK V2 environment." Videos and audios in AVI, WMV, MOV, FLV, MP4, H.264, MPEG, MPG, VOB, 3GP, 3G2, DVD, DV, MP3, WMA, and MP3 are all supported, as well as On2 VP6 and H.263 video codecs. Functions include thumbnail capture, video resizing, trimming, one processor locking (for dual-processor), desktop program and/or web-server integration.

Source: Descriptions are from Wikipedia (www.wikipedia.org) except Flash Video Encoder SDK, which is adapted from the Flash Video Tools website, and Box, which contains information from its website.

APPENDIX B

National Educational Technology Standards (NETS)

NETS for Students (NETS•S)

All K–12 students should be prepared to meet the following standards and performance indicators.

1. Creativity and Innovation

Students demonstrate creative thinking, construct knowledge, and develop innovative products and processes using technology. Students:

a. apply existing knowledge to generate new ideas, products, or processes

b. create original works as a means of personal or group expression

c. use models and simulations to explore complex systems and issues

d. identify trends and forecast possibilities

2. Communication and Collaboration

Students use digital media and environments to communicate and work collaboratively, including at a distance, to support individual learning and contribute to the learning of others. Students:

a. interact, collaborate, and publish with peers, experts, or others employing a variety of digital environments and media

b. communicate information and ideas effectively to multiple audiences using a variety of media and formats

c. develop cultural understanding and global awareness by engaging with learners of other cultures

d. contribute to project teams to produce original works or solve problems

3. Research and Information Fluency

Students apply digital tools to gather, evaluate, and use information. Students:

a. plan strategies to guide inquiry

b. locate, organize, analyze, evaluate, synthesize, and ethically use information from a variety of sources and media

c. evaluate and select information sources and digital tools based on the appropriateness to specific tasks

d. process data and report results

4. Critical Thinking, Problem Solving, and Decision Making

Students use critical-thinking skills to plan and conduct research, manage projects, solve problems, and make informed decisions using appropriate digital tools and resources. Students:

a. identify and define authentic problems and significant questions for investigation

b. plan and manage activities to develop a solution or complete a project

c. collect and analyze data to identify solutions and make informed decisions

d. use multiple processes and diverse perspectives to explore alternative solutions

5. Digital Citizenship

Students understand human, cultural, and societal issues related to technology and practice legal and ethical behavior. Students:

a. advocate and practice the safe, legal, and responsible use of information and technology

b. exhibit a positive attitude toward using technology that supports collaboration, learning, and productivity

c. demonstrate personal responsibility for lifelong learning

d. exhibit leadership for digital citizenship

6. Technology Operations and Concepts

Students demonstrate a sound understanding of technology concepts, systems, and operations. Students:

a. understand and use technology systems

b. select and use applications effectively and productively

c. troubleshoot systems and applications

d. transfer current knowledge to the learning of new technologies

© 2007 International Society for Technology in Education (ISTE), www.iste.org. All rights reserved.

NETS for Teachers (NETS·T)

All classroom teachers should be prepared to meet the following standards and performance indicators.

1. Facilitate and Inspire Student Learning and Creativity

Teachers use their knowledge of subject matter, teaching and learning, and technology to facilitate experiences that advance student learning, creativity, and innovation in both face-to-face and virtual environments. Teachers:

a. promote, support, and model creative and innovative thinking and inventiveness

b. engage students in exploring real-world issues and solving authentic problems using digital tools and resources

c. promote student reflection using collaborative tools to reveal and clarify students' conceptual understanding and thinking, planning, and creative processes

d. model collaborative knowledge construction by engaging in learning with students, colleagues, and others in face-to-face and virtual environments

2. Design and Develop Digital-Age Learning Experiences and Assessments

Teachers design, develop, and evaluate authentic learning experiences and assessments incorporating contemporary tools and resources to maximize content learning in context and to develop the knowledge, skills, and attitudes identified in the NETS•S. Teachers:

a. design or adapt relevant learning experiences that incorporate digital tools and resources to promote student learning and creativity

b. develop technology-enriched learning environments that enable all students to pursue their individual curiosities and become active participants in setting their own educational goals, managing their own learning, and assessing their own progress

c. customize and personalize learning activities to address students' diverse learning styles, working strategies, and abilities using digital tools and resources

d. provide students with multiple and varied formative and summative assessments aligned with content and technology standards and use resulting data to inform learning and teaching

3. Model Digital-Age Work and Learning

Teachers exhibit knowledge, skills, and work processes representative of an innovative professional in a global and digital society. Teachers:

a. demonstrate fluency in technology systems and the transfer of current knowledge to new technologies and situations

b. collaborate with students, peers, parents, and community members using digital tools and resources to support student success and innovation

c. communicate relevant information and ideas effectively to students, parents, and peers using a variety of digital-age media and formats

d. model and facilitate effective use of current and emerging digital tools to locate, analyze, evaluate, and use information resources to support research and learning

4. Promote and Model Digital Citizenship and Responsibility

Teachers understand local and global societal issues and responsibilities in an evolving digital culture and exhibit legal and ethical behavior in their professional practices. Teachers:

a. advocate, model, and teach safe, legal, and ethical use of digital information and technology, including respect for copyright, intellectual property, and the appropriate documentation of sources

b. address the diverse needs of all learners by using learner-centered strategies and providing equitable access to appropriate digital tools and resources

c. promote and model digital etiquette and responsible social interactions related to the use of technology and information

d. develop and model cultural understanding and global awareness by engaging with colleagues and students of other cultures using digital-age communication and collaboration tools

5. Engage in Professional Growth and Leadership

Teachers continuously improve their professional practice, model lifelong learning, and exhibit leadership in their school and professional community by promoting and demonstrating the effective use of digital tools and resources. Teachers:

a. participate in local and global learning communities to explore creative applications of technology to improve student learning

b. exhibit leadership by demonstrating a vision of technology infusion, participating in shared decision making and community building, and developing the leadership and technology skills of others

c. evaluate and reflect on current research and professional practice on a regular basis to make effective use of existing and emerging digital tools and resources in support of student learning

d. contribute to the effectiveness, vitality, and self-renewal of the teaching profession and of their school and community

NETS for Administrators (NETS·A)

All school administrators should be prepared to meet the following standards and performance indicators.

1. Visionary Leadership

Educational Administrators inspire and lead development and implementation of a shared vision for comprehensive integration of technology to promote excellence and support transformation throughout the organization. Educational Administrators:

   a. inspire and facilitate among all stakeholders a shared vision of purposeful change that maximizes use of digital-age resources to meet and exceed learning goals, support effective instructional practice, and maximize performance of district and school leaders

   b. engage in an ongoing process to develop, implement, and communicate technology-infused strategic plans aligned with a shared vision

   c. advocate on local, state, and national levels for policies, programs, and funding to support implementation of a technology-infused vision and strategic plan

2. Digital-Age Learning Culture

Educational Administrators create, promote, and sustain a dynamic, digital-age learning culture that provides a rigorous, relevant, and engaging education for all students. Educational Administrators:

   a. ensure instructional innovation focused on continuous improvement of digital-age learning

   b. model and promote the frequent and effective use of technology for learning

   c. provide learner-centered environments equipped with technology and learning resources to meet the individual, diverse needs of all learners

   d. ensure effective practice in the study of technology and its infusion across the curriculum

   e. promote and participate in local, national, and global learning communities that stimulate innovation, creativity, and digital-age collaboration

3. Excellence in Professional Practice

Educational Administrators promote an environment of professional learning and innovation that empowers educators to enhance student learning through the infusion of contemporary technologies and digital resources. Educational Administrators:

a. allocate time, resources, and access to ensure ongoing professional growth in technology fluency and integration

b. facilitate and participate in learning communities that stimulate, nurture, and support administrators, faculty, and staff in the study and use of technology

c. promote and model effective communication and collaboration among stakeholders using digital-age tools

d. stay abreast of educational research and emerging trends regarding effective use of technology and encourage evaluation of new technologies for their potential to improve student learning

4. Systemic Improvement

Educational Administrators provide digital-age leadership and management to continuously improve the organization through the effective use of information and technology resources. Educational Administrators:

a. lead purposeful change to maximize the achievement of learning goals through the appropriate use of technology and media-rich resources

b. collaborate to establish metrics, collect and analyze data, interpret results, and share findings to improve staff performance and student learning

c. recruit and retain highly competent personnel who use technology creatively and proficiently to advance academic and operational goals

d. establish and leverage strategic partnerships to support systemic improvement

e. establish and maintain a robust infrastructure for technology including integrated, interoperable technology systems to support management, operations, teaching, and learning

5. Digital Citizenship

Educational Administrators model and facilitate understanding of social, ethical, and legal issues and responsibilities related to an evolving digital culture. Educational Administrators:

   a. ensure equitable access to appropriate digital tools and resources to meet the needs of all learners

   b. promote, model, and establish policies for safe, legal, and ethical use of digital information and technology

   c. promote and model responsible social interactions related to the use of technology and information

   d. model and facilitate the development of a shared cultural understanding and involvement in global issues through the use of contemporary communication and collaboration tools

NETS for Coaches (NETS • C)

All technology coaches should be prepared to meet the following standards and performance indicators.

1. Visionary Leadership

Technology Coaches inspire and participate in the development and implementation of a shared vision for the comprehensive integration of technology to promote excellence and support transformational change throughout the instructional environment. Technology Coaches:

a. contribute to the development, communication, and implementation of a shared vision for the comprehensive use of technology to support a digital-age education for all students

b. contribute to the planning, development, communication, implementation, and evaluation of technology-infused strategic plans at the district and school levels

c. advocate for policies, procedures, programs, and funding strategies to support implementation of the shared vision represented in the school and district technology plans and guidelines

d. implement strategies for initiating and sustaining technology innovations and manage the change process in schools and classrooms

2. Teaching, Learning, and Assessments

Technology Coaches assist teachers in using technology effectively for assessing student learning, differentiating instruction, and providing rigorous, relevant, and engaging learning experiences for all students. Technology Coaches:

a. Coach teachers in and model design and implementation of technology-enhanced learning experiences addressing content standards and student technology standards

b. Coach teachers in and model design and implementation of technology-enhanced learning experiences using a variety of research-based, learner-centered instructional strategies and assessment tools to address the diverse needs and interests of all students

c. Coach teachers in and model engagement of students in local and global interdisciplinary units in which technology helps students assume professional roles, research real-world problems, collaborate with others, and produce products that are meaningful and useful to a wide audience

d. Coach teachers in and model design and implementation of technology-enhanced learning experiences emphasizing creativity, higher-order thinking skills and processes, and mental habits of mind (e.g., critical thinking, metacognition, and self-regulation)

e. Coach teachers in and model design and implementation of technology-enhanced learning experiences using differentiation, including adjusting content, process, product, and learning environment based upon student readiness levels, learning styles, interests, and personal goals

f. Coach teachers in and model incorporation of research-based best practices in instructional design when planning technology-enhanced learning experiences

g. Coach teachers in and model effective use of technology tools and resources to continuously assess student learning and technology literacy by applying a rich variety of formative and summative assessments aligned with content and student technology standards

h. Coach teachers in and model effective use of technology tools and resources to systematically collect and analyze student achievement data, interpret results, and communicate findings to improve instructional practice and maximize student learning

3. Digital-Age Learning Environments

Technology coaches create and support effective digital-age learning environments to maximize the learning of all students. Technology Coaches:

a. Model effective classroom management and collaborative learning strategies to maximize teacher and student use of digital tools and resources and access to technology-rich learning environments

b. Maintain and manage a variety of digital tools and resources for teacher and student use in technology-rich learning environments

c. Coach teachers in and model use of online and blended learning, digital content, and collaborative learning networks to support and extend student learning as well as expand opportunities and choices for online professional development for teachers and administrators

    d. Select, evaluate, and facilitate the use of adaptive and assistive technologies to support student learning

    e. Troubleshoot basic software, hardware, and connectivity problems common in digital learning environments

    f. Collaborate with teachers and administrators to select and evaluate digital tools and resources that enhance teaching and learning and are compatible with the school technology infrastructure

    g. Use digital communication and collaboration tools to communicate locally and globally with students, parents, peers, and the larger community

4. Professional Development and Program Evaluation

Technology coaches conduct needs assessments, develop technology-related professional learning programs, and evaluate the impact on instructional practice and student learning. Technology Coaches:

    a. Conduct needs assessments to inform the content and delivery of technology-related professional learning programs that result in a positive impact on student learning

    b. Design, develop, and implement technology-rich professional learning programs that model principles of adult learning and promote digital-age best practices in teaching, learning, and assessment

    c. Evaluate results of professional learning programs to determine their effectiveness on deepening teacher content knowledge, improving teacher pedagogical skills, and/or increasing student learning

5. Digital Citizenship

Technology coaches model and promote digital citizenship. Technology Coaches:

    a. Model and promote strategies for achieving equitable access to digital tools and resources and technology-related best practices for all students and teachers

    b. Model and facilitate safe, healthy, legal, and ethical uses of digital information and technologies

    c. Model and promote diversity, cultural understanding, and global awareness by using digital-age communication and collaboration tools to interact locally and globally with students, peers, parents, and the larger community

6. Content Knowledge and Professional Growth

Technology coaches demonstrate professional knowledge, skills, and dispositions in content, pedagogical, and technological areas, as well as adult learning and leadership, and are continuously deepening their knowledge and expertise. Technology Coaches:

a. Engage in continual learning to deepen content and pedagogical knowledge in technology integration and current and emerging technologies necessary to effectively implement the NETS•S and NETS•T

b. Engage in continuous learning to deepen professional knowledge, skills, and dispositions in organizational change and leadership, project management, and adult learning to improve professional practice

c. Regularly evaluate and reflect on their professional practice and dispositions to improve and strengthen their ability to effectively model and facilitate technology-enhanced learning experiences

Bibliography

AHA! Film Festival. Effingham Community Schools, Effingham, IL. Retrieved from www.effingham.k12.il.us/studentactivities/finearts/ahafilms

Azzam, A. (2009, September). Why creativity now? A conversation with Sir Ken Robinson. *Educational Leadership, 67*(1), 22–26.

Banaszewski, T. (2002). Digital storytelling finds its place in the classroom. *Multimedia Schools, 9*(1), 32–35.

Barnes, Brandon. (Ed.). (1997, October). Unleashing the power of classroom TV: A marketing and advocacy document for the use of classroom television professionals. Dallas, TX; KERA/KDTN.

Boster, F. J., Meyer, G. S., Roberto, A. J., & Inge, C. C. (2002). *A report on the effect of the Unitedstreaming application on educational performance.* Mason, MI: Cometrika, Inc., Baseline Research; Farmville, VA: Longwood University.

Bull, G., & Bell, L. (Eds.). (2010). *Teaching with digital video:* Watch, analyze, create. Eugene, OR: International Society for Technology in Education (ISTE).

Davidson, H. (2004). Meaningful digital video for every classroom—A strategic guide to integrating digital video into your lessons. *Tech & Learning*, April 5. Available at www.techlearning.com

Frazel, M. (2010). *Digital storytelling guide for educators.* Eugene, OR: International Society for Technology in Education (ISTE).

Grant, C. M. (1996, May). Professional development in a technological age: New definitions, old challenges, new resources. A paper from the research monograph, *Technology infusion and school change*, TERC. Retrieved from http://lsc-net.terc.edu/do/paper/8089/show/use_set-tech_int.html

Halverson, E. R., & Gibbons, D. (2010). "Key moments" as pedagogical windows into the digital video production process. *Journal of Computing in Teacher Education, 26*(2), 69–74.

HEC-TV. Behind the minds video specials. St. Louis, MO: Author. Retrieved from www.hectv.org/programs/series/behind-the-minds

Hicks, T. (2009). *The digital writing workshop.* Portsmouth, NH: Heinemann.

International Society for Technology in Education (ISTE). (1998, 2007), *National education technology standards for students (NETS•S)*. Eugene, OR: Author. Retrieved from www.iste.org/standards/nets-for-students

Jacobs, H. H. (Ed.). (2010). *Curriculum 21*: Essential education for a changing world. Alexandria, VA: ASCD.

Jenkins, H., with Purushotma, R., Clinton, K., Weigel, M., & Robison, A. J. (2006). *Confronting the challenges of participatory culture: Media education for the 21st century*. Chicago: The John D. and Catherine T. MacArthur Foundation. Retrieved from www.newmedialiteracies.org/wp-content/uploads/pdfs/NMLWhitePaper.pdf

Jukes, I., McCain, T., & Crockett, L. (2010). *Understanding the digital generation: Teaching and learning in the new digital landscape*. Kelowna, BC: 21st Century Fluency Project.

Katz, S. (2006). *Teach with video: A practical guide to integrate digital video projects into the subject you teach*. Seal Beach, CA: Author. (See www.teachwithvideo.com/student_movies.html for downloadable sample student handouts.)

Koehler, M., & Mishra, P. (2005). What happens when teachers design educational technology? The development of technological pedagogical content knowledge. *Journal of Educational Computing Research, 32*(2), 131–152.

Lenhart, A., & Madden, M. (2005, November). Teen content creators and consumers. Washington, DC: Pew Internet and American Life Project. Retrieved from www.pewinternet.org/Reports/2005/Teen-Content-Creators-and-Consumers.aspx

Lessig, L. (2005). *Free culture: The nature and future of creativity*. New York, NY: Penguin Books.

National Council of Teachers of English. (2008). *21st century curriculum and assessment framework*. Retrieved from www.ncte.org/positions/statements/21stcentframework

National Governors Association Center for Best Practices, & Council of Chief State School Officers. (2010). *Common core state standards for English language arts & Literacy in history/social studies, science, and technical subjects. Common core state standards for mathematics*. Retrieved from www.corestandards.org

National Writing Project, with DeVoss, D. N., Eidman-Aadahl, E., & Hicks, T. (2010). *Because digital writing matters: Improving student writing in online and multimedia environments.* San Francisco, CA: Jossey-Bass.

NetSmartz Workshop, A Program of the National Center for Missing & Exploited Children. (2011). Revealing too much. Retrieved from www.netsmartz.org/RevealingTooMuch

Ohler, J. (2007). *Digital storytelling in the classroom: New media pathways to literacy, learning and creativity.* Thousand Oaks, CA: Corwin Press.

Ohler, J. (2009, March). Orchestrating the media collage. *Educational Leadership, 66*(6). 8–13. Retrieved from www.ascd.org/publications/educational-leadership/mar09/vol66/num06/Orchestrating-the-Media-Collage.aspx

Parkway School District. (2008). K–8 Parkway tech proficiencies. Retrieved from www.pkwy.k12.mo.us/tis/index2.cfm?goToLocation=proficiencies.cfm

Parkway School District. (2009). Cyberbullying [video file]. Retrieved from www.pkwy.k12.mo.us/pdmedia/?uuid=310

Parkway School District. (2010a). Black silence [video file]. Retrieved from www.pkwy.k12.mo.us/pdmedia/?uuid=DEFA2A45-1CC4-EACA-CE0D08740B8141E4

Parkway School District. (2010b). Green eggs and ham: Miss Schilli's class [video file]. Retrieved from www.pkwy.k12.mo.us/pdmedia/?uuid=E3B1C0D4-1CC4-EACA-CEA86EB40FA16376

Partnership for 21st Century Skills. *Framework for 21st century learning.* Retrieved from www.p21.org

Pink, D. (2006). *A whole new mind.* New York, NY: Penguin Books.

Pitler, H., Hubbell, E., Kuhn, M., & Malenoski, K. (2007). *Using technology with classroom instruction that works.* Alexandria, VA: Association for Supervision & Curriculum Development.

Porter, B. (1995). Grappling's Technology and Learning Spectrum. Denver, CO: Bernajean Porter, Education Technology Planners. Retrieved from www.bjpconsulting.com/spectrum.html

Porter, B. (n.d.). *Digital storytelling across the curriculum: Finding content's deeper meaning.* Retrieved from http://creativeeducator.tech4learning.com/v05/stories/Digital_Storytelling_Across_the_Curriculum

Resnick, M., Maloney, J., Monroy-Hernandez, J., Rusk, N., Eastmond, E., Brennan, K., … Kafai, Y. (2009, November). Scratch: Programming for all. *Communications of the ACM, 52*(11), 60–67.

Robinson, K. (2006, February). Ken Robinson says schools kill creativity. *TED Talks.* Retrieved from www.ted.com/talks/lang/eng/ken_robinson_says_schools kill_creativity.html

Schuck, S., & Kearney, M. (2004, June). Digital video as a tool in research projects: Zooming in on current issues. In L. Cantoni & C. McLoughlin (Eds.), *Proceedings of ed-media 2004 world conference on educational multimedia, hypermedia and telecommunications* (pp. 2085–2092). Norfolk, VA: Association for the Advancement of Computing in Education.

Schuck, S., & Kearney, M. (2006). Capturing learning through student-generated digital video. *Australian Educational Computing, 21*(1), 15–20.

Shirkey, C. (2008). *Here comes everybody: The power of organizing without organizations.* New York, NY: Penguin Books.

Smith, G. E. (2009). *Differentiating instruction with technology in middle school classrooms.* Eugene, OR: International Society for Technology in Education (ISTE).

Taffe, S., & Gwinn, C. (2007). *Integrating literacy and technology.* New York, NY: Guilford Press.

Turan, K. (2002). *Sundance to Sarajevo: Film festivals and the world they made.* Berkeley: University of California Press.

University of Houston. (2011). *The educational uses of digital storytelling.* Houston, TX: Author. Retrieved from http://digitalstorytelling.coe.uh.edu

U.S. Department of Education, Office of Educational Technology, & National Education Technology Plan Technical Working Group. (2010). *Transforming American education: Learning powered by technology.* (National Education Technology Plan 2010). Washington, DC: Author. Retrieved from www.ed.gov/sites/default/files/netp2010.pdf

Vrasidas, C., & Glass, G. (Eds.). (2005). *Preparing teachers to teach with technology.* Greenwich, CT: Information Age Publishing.

Wesch, M. (2008, July 26). An anthropological introduction to YouTube [Video file]. Retrieved from www.youtube.com/watch?v=TPAO-lZ4_hU&

Zhao, Y. (2009). *Catching up or leading the way: American education in the age of globalization.* Alexandria, VA: ASCD.